More than Memories

The Complete Guide
For Preserving Your Family History

Edited by Julie Stephani

krause publications

700 East State Street, Iola, WI 54990-0001
Telephone (715) 445-2214

Please call or write for our free catalog of publications. Our toll-free number to place an order or obtain a free catalog is (800) 258-0929 or please use our regular business telephone (715) 445-2214 for editorial comment and further information.

Book Design by Jan Wojtech
Photography by Ross Hubbard

Library of Congress Catalog Card Number: 98-85815

ISBN 0-87341-689-9

Manufactured in the United States of America

The contents of this book is based on the *More Than Memories* TV show
produced by
David Larson Productions

Introduction

You have probably been taking pictures for many years to capture and remember the special times of your life, but what have you done to preserve those precious photos? Many of us have boxes or drawers full of our pictures and negatives, but we haven't taken the time to organize and display them like we should.

Even though I recognized the importance of preserving my photos for my family and generations to come, I wasn't doing anything about it. That is why I am so excited about the scrapbooking craze that is sweeping across the country. Suddenly, there are all kinds of wonderful ideas, supplies, and support to help me get my pictures in order . . . and have lots of fun in the process!

We call it scrapbooking because we are collecting our photos and memorabilia and are displaying them in albums. But we aren't just putting things on pages! Most of the fun is finding creative ways to arrange our photos to capture the essence of the person or event so others can share in the memories.

One of the reasons scrapbooking is so enjoyable is because we are dealing with the things that mean the most to us. Photos are of parents, children, friends, pets, nature – all of the things that give meaning to our lives. We are collecting these important images in albums which become a reflection of who we are.

Because we are learning how to preserve our photos safely, they will be passed on to future generations and our albums will become chronicles of our family history. It is sometimes difficult to see that the lives we are living today will be the history of tomorrow. That gives an even more meaningful importance to what we are doing. So begin today to capture the memories that will become a part of your family history for generations to come.

The following manufacturers' products have been used to create the sample album pages in this book.

Accu-Cut Shape and Letter Cutting Systems®

Delta Cherished Memories™ Stencils
Delta Cherished Memories™ Acid-Free Paper Paint

Elmer's® Craft Bond Paper Craft Glue Gel
Elmer's® Craft Bond Glue Stick
Elmer's® Craft Bond Glue

EK Success Ltd.
ZIG Memory System® Markers
Inkworx® Air Art Gun
Stickopotamus® Stickers

Fiskars® Paper Edgers
Fiskars® Corner Edgers
Fiskars® Personal Paper Trimmer
Fiskars® 12" Rotary Paper Trimmer
Fiskars® Circle Cutter
Fiskars® Transparent Photo Corners

Hot Off The Press, Inc.
Paper Pizazz™
Punch-Outs™

Sticker Planet™
Mrs. Grossman's™ Paper Company
The Gifted Line® Stickers
Suzy's Zoo® Stickers
Sandylion Sticker Designs™

Contents

Chapter 1: Where Do I Begin?

SEVEN EASY STEPS

❶ ORGANIZE AND PRESERVE PHOTOS

Your first task is to organize your photos, negatives, and memorabilia and store them in "archival quality" containers.

❷ BUY AND ORGANIZE SUPPLIES

Begin with the basics. You can determine what your personal needs and wishes will be once you have completed a few pages. Organize your supplies for easy access.

❸ CHOOSE A THEME AND SELECT PHOTOS

Group photos into themes or subjects. If you are planning to do more than one theme, slip additional photo groupings in labeled envelopes and work with just one theme at a time.

❹ CROP AND MAT PHOTOS

This is where you can get really creative! You have unlimited choices in how you display your photos. Use the page ideas in this book to get you started.

❺ LAYOUT PAGES

Arrange photos, memorabilia, and journaling on your pages. You can find many ideas from looking at sample pages.

❻ JOURNAL ON PAGES

Write down specific information about who and what are in the photos and tell "the rest of the story" whenever you can.

❼ PROTECT AND COLLECT PAGES

Place completed pages in protective see-through sheets. Collect pages in an album.

Organize Your Photos and Negatives

Take your treasured family history out of the shoe boxes before it is lost forever!

Whether you are putting together a scrapbook for the first time or the tenth, take time to organize the boxes and envelopes full of photos that are the fiber and framework of your personal history. Once you have your photos and negatives in order, selecting your best photos for displaying in albums will be a breeze! Even though you should save all of your photos for historical value, you will probably want to be selective when it comes to choosing what goes into your albums.

GETTING STARTED   First, gather all of your photos and negatives in one place. Select an area where you can work undisturbed until you have had time to sort through your collection. Realistically, you will probably not complete it all in one session. Set the negatives aside and begin with the photos. One thing at a time!

Pick a method of organization and separate your photos into piles. Most people prefer to arrange photos chronologically, but other options are to sort by person, season, location, or event. Many people also find it helpful to group photos based on different stages or turning points in their lives, such as childhood, school years, marriage, children, or retirement.

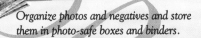

Organize photos and negatives and store them in photo-safe boxes and binders.

When you have your photos separated into groupings, label and store them in sturdy acid-free photo boxes using tabbed dividers to separate each major grouping. Larger photos and memorabilia can be organized using labeled file folders or envelopes.

Storing Negatives

One of the best methods for creating a quick and reliable system for storing and retrieving your negatives is organizing negatives in chronological order and labeling them by events.

Many photo stores and mail-order catalogs carry plastic sleeves for negatives that fit in standard three-ring binders. If you choose this method, purchase sleeves made of nonreactive plastics such as polypropylene or polyester.

Another option is to store each set of negatives in a separate acid-free envelope, labeling and filing the envelopes similar to your photos. Always store your negatives separate from your photos so you have a backup in case one of them is destroyed.

Planning Your Projects

When you have everything in order, determine what you want to focus on first. You'll be overwhelmed if you try to tackle it all. Set yourself one achievable goal at a time.

Begin with a manageable project, perhaps an album commemorating an event with a beginning and end such as a vacation or a special occasion. If you feel confident in begin-ning a family album, many scrapbook experts advise newcomers to start with the present and move forward, always keeping current. When you have extra time, work backwards through the years.

Although the organizational stage of scrapbooking might take a significant number of hours, you'll end up saving time in the long run if your photos and negatives are logically arranged and stored. Having everything in order and in one place can give you as much of a sense of accomplishment as a completed album. So tackle those boxes of photos and negatives and get yourself organized!

Adapted from an article by Carol Kauder written for Memory Makers magazine.

Preserve Your Photos & Negatives

*I*t is important to use archival-quality materials to preserve photographs. You probably have noticed that many of your old pictures have lost their color or clarity over the years. Photographs go through a chemical process in development which subjects them to natural ongoing deterioration. With careful handling, photos can last for hundreds of years, but you need to be aware of the dangers and how best to protect them from harm.

WHAT WILL DAMAGE YOUR PHOTOGRAPHS?

Even black-and-white photos are not immune to deterioration.

PHOTO DANGERS

Accidity (low PH)
PVC (polyvinylchloride which breaks
    down to form hydrochloric acid)
Humidity
Extreme temperatures
"Magnetic" albums
Dust & dirt
Sunlight
Ball-point and felt-tip pens
Fingerprints

Look for archival quality materials to protect both your photos and negatives. Archival is a term that suggests a material is permanent, durable, or chemically stable and can therefore be used safely for preservation purposes. It indicates materials are acid-free which means the item has a pH of 7.0 (neutral) or higher. pH is a measure of the concentration of hydrogen ions in a solution which is a measure of balance between acid and alkaline components of material.

Also look for materials that are "lignin free." Lignin is largely responsible for the strength and rigidity of plants, but its presence in paper is believed to contribute to chemical degradation.

Refer to the glossary on page 128 for additional information on terms having to do with the preservation of your photographs. It is important to be aware of the elements that can affect the longevity of photos in order to protect them in a safe environment for generations to come.

Album Styles

HOW DO I CHOOSE THE RIGHT ALBUM?

You should store your photos in "archival quality" albums to preserve them for the future. Albums come in a variety of sizes and types of bindings. You will probably choose more than one album style to fit your different needs.

SIZES

Albums range in size from 4"x6" to 12"x15". The two most popular and readily available sizes are 8 ½"x11" and 12"x12". You will find that many supplies such as papers, protective sheets, and border stencils are made for these two sizes, although it is easy to adapt materials to fit any size album page.

BINDINGS

Three-ring binders are popular because they are the least expensive album and the rings open easily for quick additions or changes in page arrangement; however, you will usually have to buy paper and protective sheets separately. Protective sheets have holes made to fit the rings, and sheets of paper can be inserted into the sides or top of the sheets. Some three-ring binders have "D" shaped rings which will allow the pages to lie flat.

Spiral-bound albums have a set number of pages, sometimes with protective sheets. You can not rearrange or add pages to the album, but they work well for special theme or gift albums. Advantages are that they come with very attractive covers, and they lie flat when open.

Post-bound albums have screws in the binding that allow you to add or rearrange pages, but it is not as easy to adjust as the three-ring binder. Extension posts can be purchased to increase the depth of the album for holding additional pages. The advantages are the more attractive appearance and higher quality covers.

THREE-RING BINDERS

SPIRAL-BOUND ALBUMS

POST-BOUND ALBUMS

Cutting Mat

Circle Cutter

Ruler

Eraser

X-acto Knife

Paper Trimmer

Supplies

Look at all of the supplies you can choose from to create attractive one-of-a-kind pages for your albums!

Start with the basics which you probably already have on hand. You will need **scissors**, **paper**, a **pencil**, **permanent pen**, **ruler**, and an **adhesive**. You will also need **protective sheets** to cover every page and an **album** in which to collect and display your pages.

Paper Punches

Die-Cut Shapes

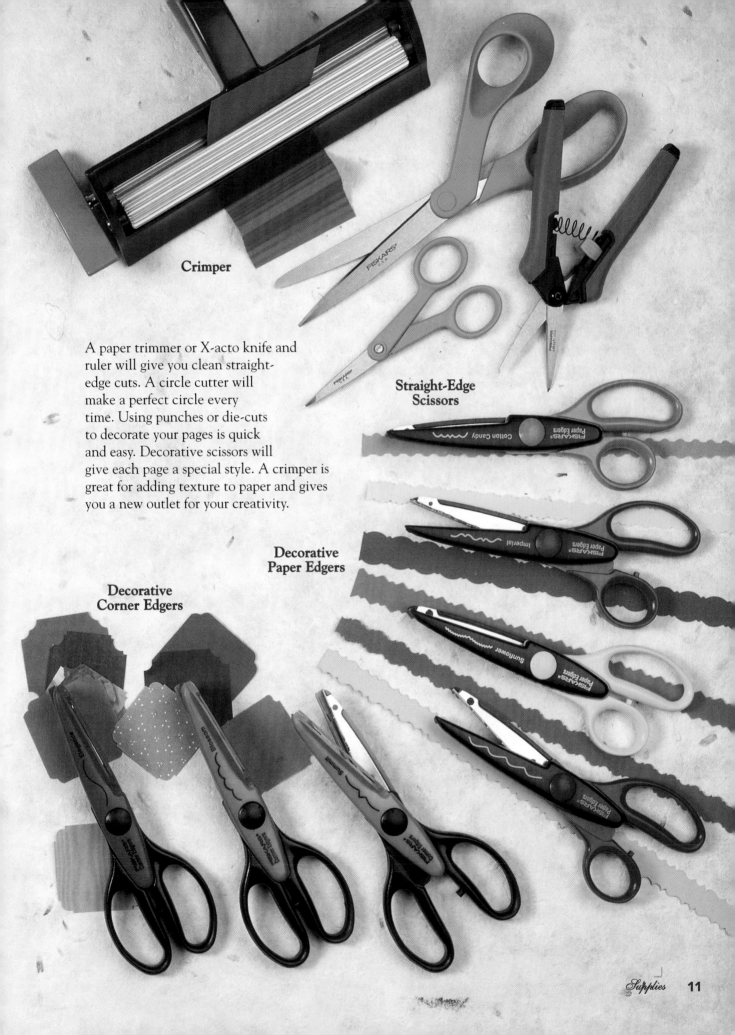

Crimper

A paper trimmer or X-acto knife and ruler will give you clean straight-edge cuts. A circle cutter will make a perfect circle every time. Using punches or die-cuts to decorate your pages is quick and easy. Decorative scissors will give each page a special style. A crimper is great for adding texture to paper and gives you a new outlet for your creativity.

Straight-Edge Scissors

Decorative Paper Edgers

Decorative Corner Edgers

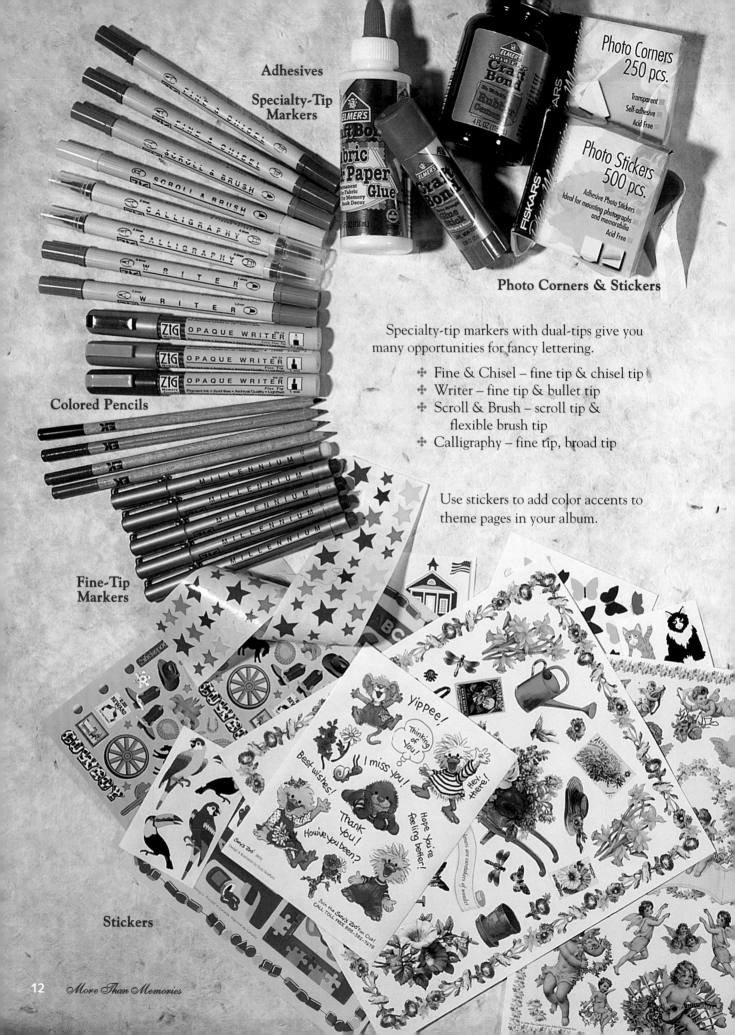

Adhesives

Specialty-Tip Markers

Photo Corners & Stickers

Colored Pencils

Fine-Tip Markers

Stickers

Specialty-tip markers with dual-tips give you many opportunities for fancy lettering.

- ✤ Fine & Chisel – fine tip & chisel tip
- ✤ Writer – fine tip & bullet tip
- ✤ Scroll & Brush – scroll tip & flexible brush tip
- ✤ Calligraphy – fine tip, broad tip

Use stickers to add color accents to theme pages in your album.

Plain & Pattern Paper

Photo corners are great for photos that you do not want to mount permanently. Photo stickers are an alternative to using glue. Plain and pattern paper come in coordinating colors. Anyone can create artistic designs with stencils and templates. Use quick-drying paper paint for no-fuss stenciling, and using rubber stamps is an easy way to decorate a page.

Stencils & Templates

Paper Paint

Rubber Stamps

Photography

Taking great photos has never been so easy! The latest cameras offer very sophisticated features that are simple to operate. Some are as easy as point and shoot! Many cameras have the option of automatic or manual operation depending on your interests and expertise. Here are some helpful hints that will give you some ideas on how to improve your photos and how to have more fun by varying your shots. Even a beginner can take great photos!

Fill the frame of your camera.

Take the same subject at different angles.

Aim your camera up.

Aim your camera down.

Get on the same level as children.

Take the same shot from
different distances.

Try the same shot both verti-
cally and horizontally. (Note
that natural foliage makes a
good background.)

To avoid red eyes on
people and blue/gold
eyes on animals,
increase the surrounding
light if possible, have
subject turn slightly
away from the camera,
or increase the distance
between you and your
subject. After the fact,
use a "Red Eye" or "Pet
Eye" pen to change eyes
to a more natural color.

Be on the lookout for special images that are rare treasures.

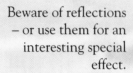

Beware of reflections – or use them for an interesting special effect.

Take a series of pictures, one after another, to capture a reaction at a special moment.

Frame in a scenery shot with something in the foreground. Tree branches are a natural!

For a special shot (like Christmas cards), take numerous shots, then choose the best one.

Catch action shots whenever you can.

When taking shots of recognizable landmarks, monuments, etc., look for an angle that gives a different perspective.

Cropping

WHAT DOES CROPPING MEAN?

It simply means cutting a photograph.

WHY DO YOU CROP?

Cropping focuses on a subject by cutting away the unimportant or distracting background around it.

WHEN DO YOU CROP?

Only crop when necessary to improve the focus of the photo. Do it sparingly. Backgrounds in photos often show details that are important to the time and place of the photo.

Needs Cropping

Cropped Too Much

Just Right

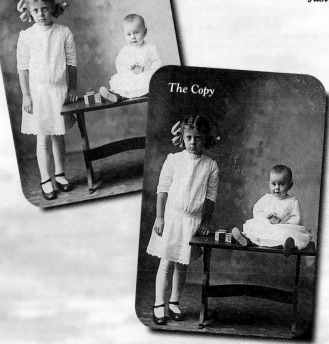

The Original

The Copy

Do not cut any photo unless you have a duplicate or a way to copy the photo. Make a color copy of one-of-a-kind photos and only crop the copy. Color copies look very similar to the original and work especially well for black and white or sepia-tone (brown-tone) photos. Sometimes copies even improve the contrast. Practice cropping on throwaway photos before you begin working with your treasured ones.

HOW DO YOU CROP?

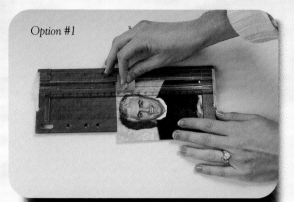

Option #1

To make a straight cut . . .

❶ use a paper cutter . . .

❷ use an x-acto knife and ruler . . .

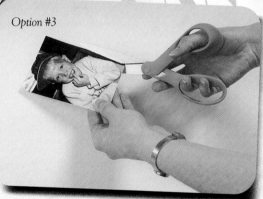

Option #2

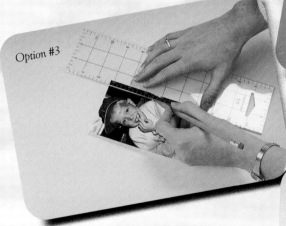

Option #3

❸ draw lines on photo with a pencil and ruler and cut INSIDE the lines with a scissors. Hold scissors still and cut while turning the photo.

Option #3

For curved lines and shapes, use a plastic see-through template (pattern). Position template over photo and trace around shape with a pencil. Cut photo INSIDE lines with knife or scissors.

CROPPING TIPS

Formal photos look best when cut into ovals or rectangles.

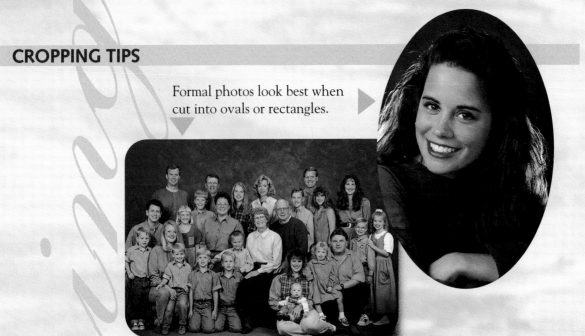

Save fun shapes for more informal photos. Use templates to compliment pages with special themes. An unusual shape will highlight a photo, drawing attention to it.

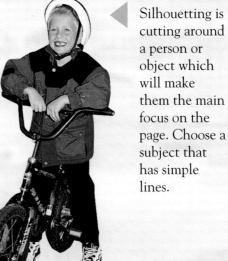

Silhouetting is cutting around a person or object which will make them the main focus on the page. Choose a subject that has simple lines.

Bumping is cutting around ONLY ONE PART of a person or an object.

Crop before you shoot! To eliminate unwanted background, step closer to your subject before taking the picture. (A zoom lens will save you time and steps in catching a moment at the perfect distance.)

See how different the same photo can look when it is cropped in a variety of shapes.

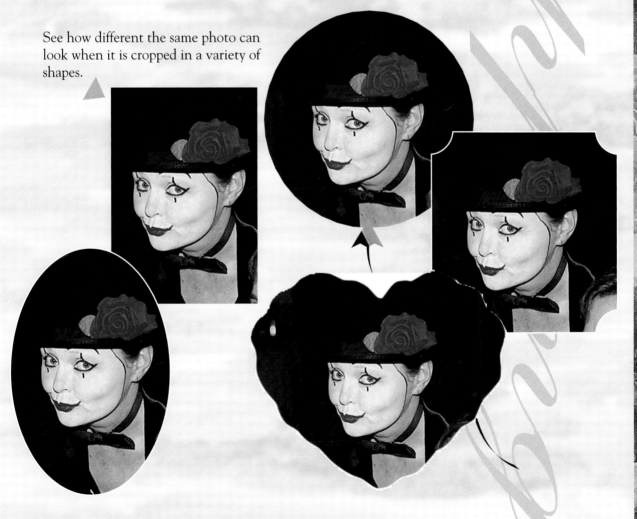

Matting

To make a basic single mat, glue photo on plain or printed paper, leaving a paper border showing along the edges. Draw a light pencil line for a guide if you need one. Cut around photo, leaving a 1/8" to 1/2" border. Use either a straight-edged or decorative-edged scissors. Erase pencil line if necessary.

Repeat above step for additional layers of mats, varying straight and decorative edges. Vary the widths of the mats, too. Make as many layers as you want!

Cut around photo with decorative-edged scissors before gluing photo on mat. It will look like the inside of the mat has a pattern edge. Vary straight and decorative edges for additional mats.

Mix up your mat shapes. Ovals and circles look good with rectangles and squares. Use your imagination! Punch out shapes from matching paper to decorate the corners.

Turn mats so they are not straight with the photo.

Cut just the corners of photos and mats using decorative-edged scissors.

Create a shadow by moving the outside mat to one side of the photo or the other. Cut the shadow the same shape as the largest photo mat. The light source should be the same for all of the pictures on one page, so place shadows in the same position for all photos (all to the right, all to the bottom, etc.).

Die-cuts (precut shapes) make great theme mats.

Paint a stenciled mat around a photo.

Decorate a mat with stickers.

Layouts

WHAT IS A LAYOUT?

It is the arrangement of type and art on paper. In your album, it is the arrangement of photos, lettering, paper, die-cuts, stickers, etc. on a page.

WHAT MAKES A GOOD LAYOUT?

❶ A layout should accomplish its purpose.

In an album you are telling a story with pictures and words. You want to capture an image, a moment in time, or an event so that the person looking at the page can share in the memory. When you complete a page ask the question, "Did I accomplish this?"

❷ A layout should be organized.

An effective layout should help the person looking at your album get through each page easily. It needs a focal point or a main point of interest. Choose what should be seen first. Decide how you will make it stand out from everything else. What will be next? Continue arranging and emphasizing the pieces on the page until everything is seen and understood. The upper left corner is usually looked at first, and eyes naturally go from left to right.

❸ A layout should be attractive.

Make the arrangement on each page interesting. Enlarge a photo of importance, or put a bright color behind it. Photos cropped in ovals or shapes will draw attention. Tilt an image or vary the sizes of images and lettering. Choose papers with interesting designs and textures. Create contrast with light and dark colors next to each other.

There is no one right way to make a good layout, but it should accomplish what you want it to do. It should be organized, setting a visual path for the person looking at it, and it should be attractive to draw a person's attention to it. When you complete a page, ask yourself three questions. "Does it work?" "Is it organized?" "Is it attractive?" If you answer "yes" to all three questions, you have a good layout!

Journaling

Telling the story behind the photos in your albums is one of the most important things you can do to pass down your family history to future generations. The more information you include, the more valuable each page becomes. To include the basic information, answer the traditional news story questions Who? What? When? Where? Why? How? Include at least the facts and then add the heartfelt details and descriptions to make your journaling more interesting and meaningful to those who want to share your special memories.

Make sure you allow enough room on your pages for your writing. You can make pocket pages or attach envelopes to use for storing longer stories. Here are three examples of journaling the same photo.

Answer the basic questions in a traditional news story.

Give additional information to the facts in a "bullet" form.

Tell a descriptive story that captures the story behind the photo.

Protect Photo Pages

When pages are complete, place them in protective see-through sheets which are acid-free. Protective sheets come in top-loading and side-loading styles. They vary from lightweight to heavyweight in thickness and are punched with three holes to fit into three-ring binders or albums.

The *Gift* of *Family*

SUPPLIES

❖ Paper Pizazz: Cream, light blue, dark blue
   (Solid Muted)
❖ Fiskars Paper Edger: Deckle

❖ Elmer's Craft Bond Glue Stick

INSTRUCTIONS

Use colored paper to represent family blood-lines, and you can see family connections at a glance. The mother's photos are matted with light blue, and the father's are matted with dark blue. Their son's photos are matted with a combination of light and dark blue. Assign different colors to each family branch. Include more than just photos on the pages. Check each item with a pH testing pen. If acidity is not within safe levels, the item can be sprayed with a de-acidification spray.

Design by Jane Casebolt for *Memory Makers*

Vera Florence

Dorothy Mae
Vera Florence

July, 1915

1932

Vera Florence
Leeman

SUPPLIES

✤ Paper Pizazz: Flower & lace paper (Romantic)
  Cream, blue, mauve (Solid Muted)
  Laser-cut lace (Romantic)
  Vintage date (Black & White)

✤ Fiskars: Corner Edger - Nostalgia
    Paper Edger - Majestic
✤ ZIG MS marker: Black Millenium
✤ Mrs. Grossman's stickers: Flowers, doves,
    heart
✤ Elmer's Paper Craft Glue Gel

INSTRUCTIONS

Capture the romantic spirit of times gone by with flowers and lace. Write about the people in the photos and slip the special memories into an envelope. This envelope contains a chronological history of Vera's life as well as a special memory piece written by her sister Dorothy about the day Vera was born. To make the envelope, fold a full page into thirds. Trace the flap of a standard envelope on top edge of paper. Cut flap with paper edgers. The cut-lace border and vintage stickers add an elegant touch to the page.

Design by Julie Stephani for Krause Publicatons

Martin's *Christmas*

SUPPLIES

✤ Paper Pizazz: Black & white swirl paper
   (Black & White)
   Red moire paper (Black & White)
   Gold metallic paper (Metallic)
   Green, black papers (Solid Jewel Tones)
✤ Fiskars Paper Edger: Deckle
✤ ZIG MS marker: Gold Opaque Writer
✤ Accu-Cut die-cuts: Holly & berries
✤ Elmer's Craft Bond Paper Glue Gel

INSTRUCTIONS

Special portraits deserve special treatment such as this triple-matted photo. If you are hesitant about cutting one-of-a-kind older photos, just make a color copy onto acid-free, lignin-free paper. The gold is a perfect accent on the die-cut holly leaves and dots on the berries. The journaling frame is also matted on gold paper, and the narrow green mat ties in with the green holly leaves at the top of the page. Design by Becky Goughnour for Hot Off The Press

How did we meet?

SUPPLIES

✤ FISKARS Paper Edgers: Ripple, Colonial
✤ ZIG MS marker: Black Millinium
✤ Cardstock: Red, white, blue, gold
✤ Alphabet stickers
✤ Elmer's Craft Bond Glue Stick

INSTRUCTIONS

Patriotic colors of red white and blue are a great choice for a background because this is the cover page of a section in an album that tells about two people's lives during World War II.

The triple-matted photos stand out from the bold background. Papers are pieced together to fit the 12"x12" page, but it isn't noticeable.

Design by Joyce Schweitzer for *Memory Makers*

Season's Greetings

SUPPLIES

- Paper Pizazz: Red, blue paper (School Days)
- Fiskars: Corner Edger: Nostalgia
   Decorative Scrapbook Kit, (Christmas)
   Transparent Photo Corners
   Personal Paper Trimmer
- ZIG MS marker: Black Millenium
- Elmer's Craft Bond Fabric & Paper Glue

INSTRUCTIONS

Old treasured photos can be safely mounted using photo corners. The paper corners shown on the photos are glued onto the photo corners, not the photo. For outside mat, cut off corners.

Cut four corners from contrast color and glue on each corner leaving a space. Outline with dots and dashes around outside mat and add journaling. Design from Fiskars Inc.

Bess and her sisters

SUPPLIES

- Paper Pizazz: Wooded paper (Vacation)
   Green paper (Outdoors)
   Lime green, yellow paper (Plain Brights)
   Log cabin Punch-Out
- Fiskars Paper Edger: Leaf
- ZIG MS marker: Black Millenium
- Pine tree stamp
- Elmer's Craft Bond Paper Craft Glue

INSTRUCTIONS

Become your family historian! This page was put together after four of the Cook sisters were photographed and interviewed about their family remembrances when they were together at a reunion in the north woods of Minnesota.

Their chronological family history, beginning with Bess' journey over the Oklahoma prairie in a covered wagon, is enclosed in the envelope. The wooded theme captures the setting of their childhood. Design by Julie Stephani for Krause Publications

1909 Wedding

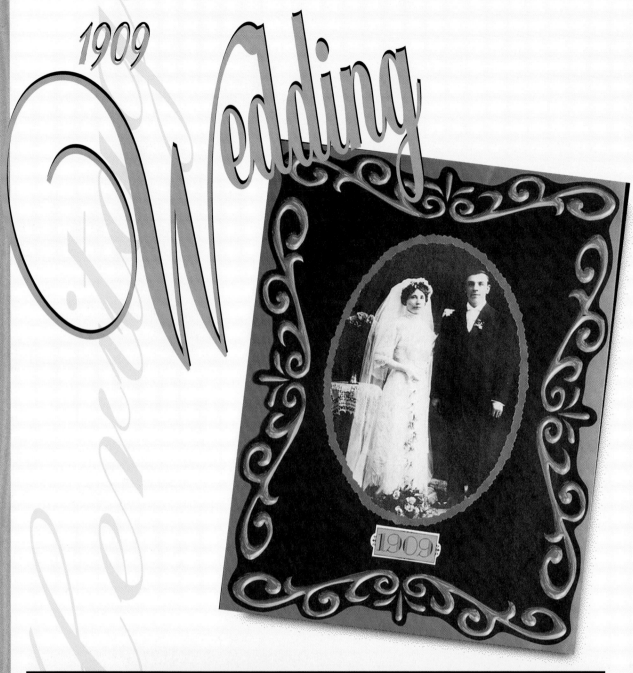

SUPPLIES

❖ Paper Pizazz: Gold stencil paper
   (Black & White)
   Gold metallic paper (Metallic)
   1909 cutout (Black & White)

❖ Fiskars Paper Edger: Deckle
❖ Elmer's Paper Craft Gel

INSTRUCTIONS

The gold stencil paper could be used by itself with the photo matted once on gold metallic paper to duplicate the gold in the stencil. As shown here, you can cut around the outside of the stencil and glue it onto another sheet of gold paper for a fancy yet easy-to-do mat. The date is simply cut out and glued on the page.

Design by Katie Hacker for Hot Off The Press

Helen Janis

SUPPLIES

- Paper Pizazz: Vintage Lace paper (Pretty)
  Lavender paper (Solid Muted)
  Ivory paper (Plain Pastel)
- Fiskars Paper Edger: Nostalgia
- ZIG MS markers: Ivory Opaque Writer, Extra Fine
  Grape Opaque Writer, Chisel
- Elmer's Craft Bond Glue Stick

INSTRUCTIONS

Letter headline on separate piece of lavender paper with grape Chisel tip Opaque Writer, following "Script" alphabet. By doing your lettering on a smaller piece of paper, you won't risk ruining a whole sheet if you make a mistake.

Add accent dots to initial letters and around mat. For outside purple border, use grape Chisel Opaque Writer to line edge of page.

Design by Carol Snyder for EK Success

Jacob & Lisa Malmstrom

Jacob & Lisa Malmstrom

Front Row:
- Lisa Person
  Born: 5 Jun 1829 - Lyby, Sweden
- Clarice Malmstrom
  Born: 5 Jan 1867 - West Jordan, UT
- Niel Jacob Malmstrom
  Born: 14 Mar 1869 - West Jordan, UT
- Alma Ephriam Malmstrom
  Born: 16 Aug 1871 - West Jordan, UT
- Jacob Malmstrom
  Born: 26 Feb 1824 - Sweden

Back Row:
- John Malmstrom
  Born: Jul 1852 - Lund, Sweden
- Peter Malmstrom
  Born: 10 Sept 1860 - West Jordan, UT
- Ellen Sophia Malmstrom Bateman
  Born: 1862 - West Jordan, UT
- Joseph Malmstrom
  Born: 1865 - West Jordan, UT
- Matilda Malmstrom Jacobsen
  Born: 25 Mar 1855 - Sweden

SUPPLIES

✤ Paper Pizazz : Gray marbled paper (Black & White)
   Mauve paper (Solid Muted)
   Silver moiré paper
✤ Fiskars Paper Edger: Heartbeat

✤ ZIG MS markers: Opaque Writer, Extra Fine — Silver, black
   Silver Opaque Writer, Chisel
   Black Writer
✤ Elmer's Craft Bond Glue Stick

INSTRUCTIONS

Letter family name and historical information on a separate piece of mauve paper, following "Script" alphabet. Use silver chisel Opaque Writer for large name and both silver and black extra fine Opaque Writers for detail information. Cut mauve corners and glue on top corners of page. Use silver extra-fine Opaque Writer to add accent dots to mat and corners.

Design by Carol Snyder for EK Success

Aa Bb Cc Dd

Ee Ff Gg Hh

Ii Jj Kk Ll

Mm Nn Oo

Pp Qq Rr Ss

Tt Uu Vv W

Xx Yy Zz

House in Winter

4909
Daniel
Drive

Winter
1998

SUPPLIES

❖ Paper Pizazz: Blue, white, black
❖ Fiskars Paper Edger: Dragonback

❖ ZIG MS markers: Black Writer
      Black Millenium
❖ Elmer's Craft Bond Glue Stick

INSTRUCTIONS

Don't forget to take pictures of your house as well as your family! Include different views in a grouping on one page. The stark bold colors of winter are accented by the black and white mats. Blue is always a good background for winter pictures. It brings out the blue cast in the shadows of the snow. Simple dots and lines define the edges of the white mat.

Design by Julie Stephani for Krause Publications

OUR FAMILY RELATIONS

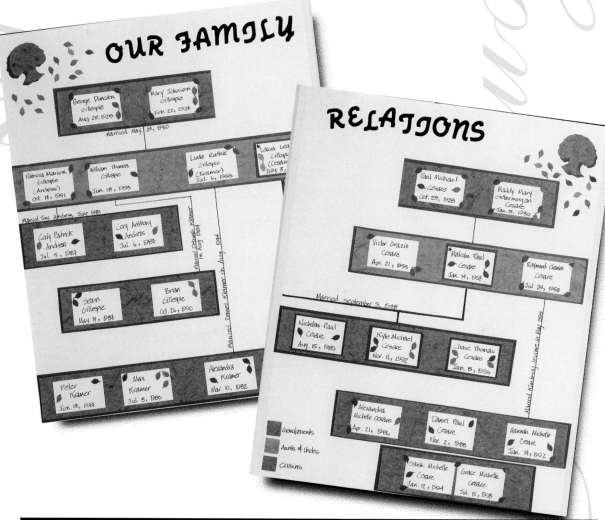

SUPPLIES

❖ Paper Pizazz: Green, purple, pink
    (Handmade)
❖ ZIG MS marker: Black Writer

❖ Punches: Tree, small leaf
❖ Alphabet stickers
❖ Elmer's Craft Bond Glue Stick

INSTRUCTIONS

Color-coding your family tree is a good way to understand family relationships at a glance. It makes it easy to explain to children how they fit into the picture. The green paper is used for grandparents, pink for aunts and uncles, and purple for cousins. The immediate family is highlighted by placing a piece of coordinating solid paper behind each name.

Design by Laura Cesare for *Memory Makers* magazine

OUR FAMILY
Garden

- Paper Pizazz: Yellow, red
    (Plain Brights)
- ZIG MS markers:
    1.2mm Writers - Blue, green,
       yellow, pink
    .05 Millenium, Black
    Clean Color, #40 Green
- Colored pencils: Primary Colors,
    Pastel Colors
- Suzy's stickers: Suzy's Blooms
    Suzy & Friends
    Flower Border Suzy
- Elmer's Craft Bond Glue Stick

INSTRUCTIONS

Cut pictures in circles and mat with bright colors. Draw flowers and leaves on a separate sheet of paper. Color with colored pencils and cut out. Arrange flowers and leaves on page and glue down. Glue photos on center of flowers. Draw grass at bottom of page with markers and place sticker characters along grass. Add dot squiggles to bee and bug. Draw cloud outline across top of page and color with pastel blue pencil above cloud line. Print title, embellishing open letters and "dot" of the letter "i" with markers.

Design by Heidi Geffen for Sticker Planet

MUG

SUPPLIES

- ZIG MS markers: Orange Writer
- Sticker Planet sticker: Flower Border Suzy
    Friendly Sentiments
- Sticker Planet plastic mug

INSTRUCTIONS

Remove paper liner from mug. Press border of flowers close to bottom of paper. Place characters in grass and have mouse jumping in the air. Write name at top. Insert paper liner back into mug with seam behind the handle. Snap lid on mug.

Design by Heidi Geffen for Sticker Planet

Vinyl Carrying Cases

JAKE'S SUPPLIES

✤ ZIG MS Opaque writers: Fine-point - Holly berry, blue
✤ Sticker Planet large vinyl carrying case: Yellow
✤ Sticker Planet stickers: Vacation & Travel, Tools, Sports, Back-to-School

NIKKI'S SUPPLIES

✤ Sticker Planet large vinyl carrying case: Red
  Sticker Planet stickers: Suzy & Friends
✤ ZIG MS Opaque writers: Fine-point - Red, yellow

INSTRUCTIONS

Decorate totes that are great for kids who are doing scrapbooking! They're the perfect size for stickers, glue, markers, and kids' scissors. It's never too soon to start organizing your supplies!

Write a name on front of the tote to personalize it for a special child. Decorate with stickers.

Designs by Heidi Geffen for Sticker Planet

HOME IS WHERE THE HEART IS

SUPPLIES

✤ Paper Pizazz: Stick drawings (School Days)
✤ Fiskars: Rotary Paper Trimmer
    Victorian and Tiara Blades, 45mm
    Corner Edger - Celestial
    8" Bent Scissors
✤ Elmer's Craft Bond Paper Glue

INSTRUCTIONS

You can turn an 8½"x11" paper into an 11" square simply by adding strips of paper! Cut four 2"x11" green strips. Trim one long edge with Victorian paper trimmer. Glue together to form an 11" square frame. Miter the corners for a more finished look. Position over 8½"x 11" patterned paper to make an 11" square. Cut four 1/2"x11" yellow strips. Trim long edges with Tiara paper trimmer. Glue one yellow strip down center of each green strip. Mount photos on contrasting paper and trim edges of mat with Victorian paper trimmer. Cut mats with Celestial corner edger.

Design from Fiskars Inc.

BIKE DUDES

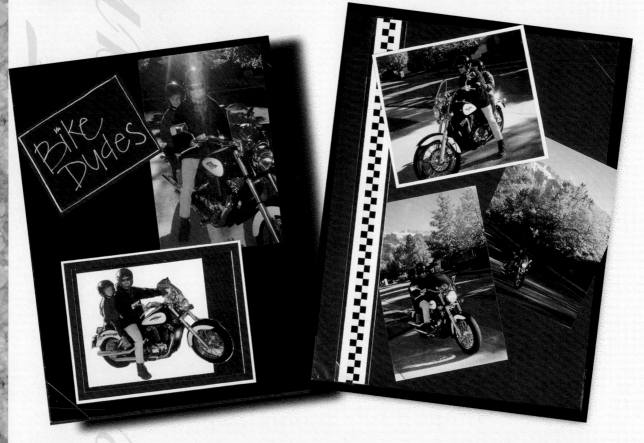

SUPPLIES

✤ ZIG MS marker: Silver Opaque writer
✤ Silver and black shiny paper
✤ Black and white cardstock

✤ Mrs. Grossman's checked border stickers
✤ Clear plastic corner mounts
✤ Elmer's Craft Bond Paper Glue

INSTRUCTIONS

What a dramatic black and white page! Look at all of the creative touches. The focus photograph is cropped as a silhouette. Metallic silver paper is used for matting. White and black are used to create balance between the two pages. Shiny black and plain black paper are trimmed 1/2" on all sides. Using large plastic corner mounts, the shiny paper is mounted on a full sheet of plain paper, and the plain paper is mounted on a full sheet of shiny paper. A checked border sticker is mounted on white then silver paper. On the left page, photographs are tilted and overlapped, having one photo off the edge of the page for added interest. Write title in silver on black rectangle. Draw silver line around border of rectangle.

Design from *Creating Keepsake* magazine

Sweet Pete Polishes

Cousin Maddie in St. George, Utah!

↑ Showing off red, white and blue nails with **Barbara Tanner**

Peter Age 4

Mom's daily **Manicure** →

My Specialty Colors
- Sunny Geranium
- Cancun Fiesta
- Ambrosia
- Aegean Coral

Don't forget the... pedicure

Sweet Pete... Polishes

SUPPLIES

✤ ZIG MS markers: Black Writer
   Millenium: Red, black
✤ Red and white striped paper
✤ Cardstock: Red, tan and white

✤ Accu-Cut die-cut: Nail polish bottle
✤ Delta Cherished Memories red paper paint
✤ Elmer's Craft Bond Paper Glue

INSTRUCTIONS

Look what you can do if you collect pictures on the same theme over a period of time. One photo is cut in a circle and matted on red for a main focus. The child and adult hands are a good balance on the two pages. Child's nails are painted red, and the adult's nails are cut from red cardstock. What a clever use of solid and striped paper, and the journaling is varied and creative, too!

Design from Creating Keepsakes *magazine*

makin' cookies

SUPPLIES

- Paper Pizazz: Blue, red, green
- Fiskars Paper Edger: Stamp
- ZIG MS markers: Black writer
    Millenium - Black, red
- Cookie cutters
- Delta Paper Paints: Blue, red, green
- Paper towel
- Paintbrush
- Elmer's Craft Bond Paper Glue

INSTRUCTIONS

Cookie-cutter outlines are a great accent for pages with special themes – especially anything to do with baking cookies! Apply paint along edges of cutter. Dab on paper towel to remove excess paint and press cutter on page. Draw faces, hair, and hearts or leave them plain.

Design by Julie Stephani for Krause Publications

HOMECOMING

SUPPLIES

- Paper Pizazz: White
- ZIG MS markers:
    Writer - Blue
    Calligraphy - Blue
    Millenium, .05 -
    Black, orange, red
- Suzy's Zoo stickers:
    Hugging Bears
    Little Mouse
    Suzy with Butterflies
    Suzy with Leaves
    Suzy with Fruit Basket
    Emily with Leaves
    Fall Harvest
- Elmer's Craft Bond
    Glue Stick

INSTRUCTIONS

When using stickers, be sure they interact with other things on the page. If stickers are peeking out from behind a photo, position sticker first and press both on page together. Create gingham borders on a separate sheet of paper using calligraphy marker. Trim into strips and arrange borders in corners of page and below photos.

Create dialogue balloon and banner on a separate sheet of paper. Add words, cut out, and glue on photos. Print title and other photo journaling. Add sticker characters around photos. Create border with leaves and acorns, using red and orange pens to make falling leaf squiggles.

Design by Heidi Geffen for Sticker Planet

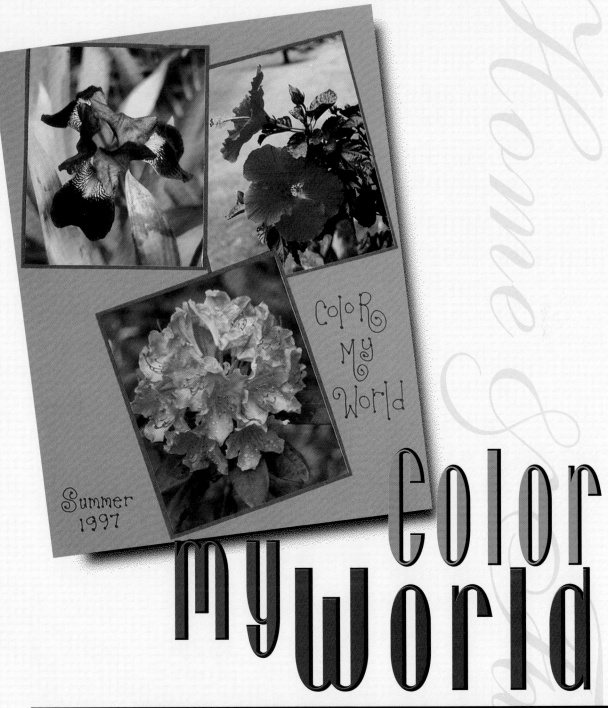

Color
My
World

Summer
1997

color
my
world

SUPPLIES

✤ Paper Pizazz: Green, brown
✤ ZIG MS marker: Black Writer

✤ Elmer's Craft Bond Glue Stick

INSTRUCTIONS

When you have beautiful pictures of flowers, keep it simple. Set off the photos with single mats and choose colors that enhance the subjects. The layout should be simple, too. The photos are slightly tilted and barely overlap each other to create a flow from one to the other on the page.

Design by Julie Stephani for Krause Publications

Family Tree

- Paper Pizazz: Leaf paper (Handmade) Tan, Light brown, dark green (Solid Muted)
- Fiskars Paper Edger: Leaf
- ZIG MS markers: Calligraphy - Black, brown Black Writer
- Stickopotamus stickers: Fall leaves
- Elmer's Craft Bond Paper Glue

INSTRUCTIONS

This page gives new meaning to "family tree!" The tree is cut from light brown paper and bark details are added lightly with brown Calligraphy marker. People are cropped, leaving a small edge of background. The oval photo at bottom of tree is double matted with a leaf print and dark green solid paper. The headline and journaling are printed with brown and black Calligraphy markers, using the "Log Cabin" alphabet. Use black Calligraphy marker to add checkerboard accents for page border and hash marks throughout page. Add fall leaf stickers for color accents.

Design by Carol Snyder for EK Success

Remember -- you can add shadow lines to any letter styles!

LOG CABIN... USE THE BROAD TIP WITH A RULER TO DRAW STRAIGHT LINES (WOOD BOARDS) THAT INTERSECT INTO THE SHAPE OF EACH LETTER. ··· USE THE NARROW TIP TO ADD DIAMONDS (NAILS) TO HOLD LETTERS TOGETHER. ··· A FUN AND EASY LETTERING STYLE FOR OUTDOORS, SCOUTING, CONSTRUCTION, CAMPING, ETC. CREATE SMALLER LETTERS WITH NARROW TIP.

Chapter 4: Cropping Parties

The quilting bees of the past have turned into the cropping parties of the present! Getting together with friends and family to work on memory pages together has become one of the most rewarding aspects of scrapbooking. It is a time to share ideas and supplies and get advice on how to do a new technique. People come to be inspired and to be encouraged by each other. It is a wonderful opportunity to enjoy socializing and be productive at the same time. Cropping parties can be as informal as calling a friend or two and asking them over for an after-noon of scrapbooking. Some enthusiasts have organized on-going cropping parties that meet on a regular basis. If you like to plan theme parties, complete with invitations, having a cropping party may be your choice. Remember that people get together to work on their albums, so don't have too many activities get in the way. Also, keep food and drink away from your work area when you are working on pages. Whatever type of get-together you decide to have, get it organized as soon as possible and let the fun begin!

PICNIC pot luck

SUPPLIES

- Paper Pizazz: Tablecloth (Outdoors)
- Fiskars Paper Edger: Pinking
- ZIG MS marker: Black Writer
- Accu-Cut die-cuts: Silver grill
      Black ants
- Baby rick rack: Yellow, black
- Yellow 1/4" wide satin ribbon, 10 inches
- Red gingham fabric
- Small wicker basket
- Red plates & cups
- Elmer's Craft Bond Paper Glue
- White cardstock

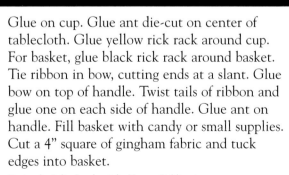

INSTRUCTIONS

For invitations, fold picnic tablecloth paper in half. Cut paper in half. Cut sides with the paper edger. Draw dash lines along edge of paper. Write message on front of paper with hotdog design. On other paper, glue grill die cut on front. Cut two clouds of smoke from white paper and glue above grill. Write message on smoke cloud. Write information inside of invitation.

For cup, cut a 2"x2 1/2" piece from tablecloth paper. Draw dash lines along edge of paper.

Glue on cup. Glue ant die-cut on center of tablecloth. Glue yellow rick rack around cup. For basket, glue black rick rack around basket. Tie ribbon in bow, cutting ends at a slant. Glue bow on top of handle. Twist tails of ribbon and glue one on each side of handle. Glue ant on handle. Fill basket with candy or small supplies. Cut a 4" square of gingham fabric and tuck edges into basket.

Design by Julie Stephani for Krause Publications

Patchwork Stocking

SUPPLIES

- Paper Pizazz: Christmas themes
- Fiskars Paper Edgers: Notch, Deckle
- ZIG MS markers: Writers - Black, red
    Black Millenium
- Cardstock: Red, white
- Elmer's Craft Bond Glue Stick

INSTRUCTIONS

Show your party guests a great way to use small leftover pieces of paper by making a crazy-patch design. The stocking is a pocket, too! Draw stocking shape on cardstock paper and cut out. Place scraps of leftover paper on stocking, cutting edges with Notch paper edger. Cut pictures to fit toe, heel, and one patch of stocking. Mat with red paper. Glue pieces in place. Draw stitching lines with black Writer. Turn stocking over and trim paper even with stocking. Draw cuff on white cardstock and cut out with Deckle paper edger. Mat with red paper and edge in same way. Glue cuff on top of stocking. Write child's name and date with Millenium marker. Add red dot accents. To make a pocket, apply glue close to the edge of the stocking, leaving top open.

Design from Fiskars, Inc.

HORSIN' AROUND

Marty & Sass. 2nd place

Horsin' Around

SUPPLIES

- Paper Pizazz: Denim paper (Country)
  Barnwood paper (Country)
  Oatmeal paper (Solid Muted)
  Blue, green, yellow, orange papers
  "Horsin' Around (Sayings Punch-Outs)
- Fiskars: Paper Edger - Deckle
  Paper Punch - Star
- ZIG MS marker: Black Millennium
- Accu-Cut die-cuts: Boot, fence
- Elmer's Craft Bond Glue

INSTRUCTIONS

Cut a large photo to create a scene. The fence is die cut from paper that looks like wood. It was matted on brown and then glued over bottom of photo. Photos are double matted on plain and then oatmeal paper. The two offset boots add to the western theme and work great for journaling. Punched stars accent the simple triangle corners.

Design by Katie Hacker for Hot Off the Press

Lights, Camera, Action

SUPPLIES

- Paper Pizazz: Black, red, yellow, white
- Fiskars paper Edger: Jigsaw
- ZIG MS markers: Black Scroll & Brush
    Black Writer
    White Opaque Writer, extra fine
    Red Millennium, .03
- Stickopotamus stickers: "Cinema"
- Elmer's Craft Bond Glue Stick

INSTRUCTIONS

With black Scroll & Brush, print titles, using the "Film It" alphabet. Add accent dash marks with red Millennium marker. Cut around letters of title, leaving a 1/8" border. Mat photos leaving room on mat at top or bottom to journal with black Writer. Cut all mat edges with Jigsaw paper edger. Cut a white rectangle for journaling. Glue pieces on black paper. Add triple dot doodles with white Opaque Writer. Add stickers for accents.

Design by Carol Snyder for EK Success

SUPPLIES

- Paper Pizazz: Ticket stubs paper (Teen Years) Red, purple, yellow, orange, white, blue
- Fiskars Paper Edger: Colonial
- ZIG MS markers: Scroll & Brush- red, black, violet, orange Black Millenium, .01
- Accu-Cut die-cuts: Ticket stubs
- Elmer's Craft Bond Glue Stick

INSTRUCTIONS

Use this idea for a movie or theater-theme party. Show how you can create a page to look like a production marquee. Letter the title of the production on white paper, using the "Film It" alphabet and the Scroll & Brush markers. Mat on orange paper and cut with Colonial paper edger. Draw hearts and border lines with black and orange markers. Write names on ticket stub die-cuts. Cut a white oval for journaling and trim with paper edger. Double mat a photo.

Design by Carol Snyder for EK Success

A a B b C c D d
E e F f G g H h I i
J j K k L l M m
n N O o P p Q q R
P S s T t U u V
W w X x Y y Z z

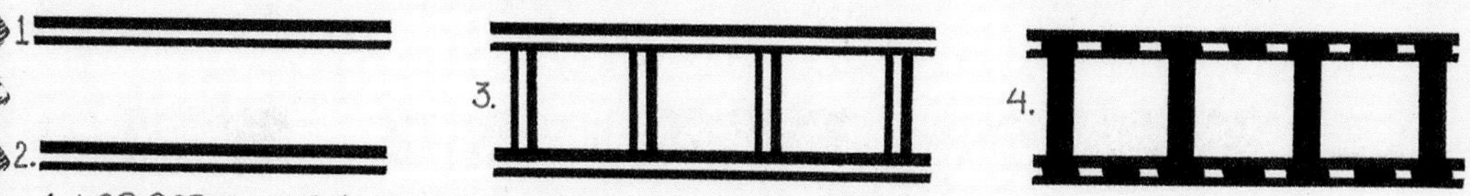

1. USE SCROLL TIP & RULER TO DRAW A LONG HORIZONTAL LINE. 2. DRAW SECOND LINE ABOUT ONE INCH BELOW. 3. DRAW VERTICAL LINES ABOUT ONE INCH APART FOR "LADDER." 4. USE BRUSH TIP TO FILL IN FOR "FILMSTRIP."

Chapter 5 : Holidays

SUPPLIES

- Paper Pizazz: Plaid paper (Ho Ho Ho!)
- Fiskars: Paper Edger - Majestic
  Paper Crimper
- ZIG MS markers: Writers - Black, green, red
  Opaque: Silver, gold
- ZIG MS colored pencils: primary colors
- Cardstock: Red, white, green
- Accu-Cut die-cuts: Ornaments
- The Gifted Line stickers: Santa
- Elmer's Craft Bond Paper Glue

INSTRUCTIONS

You will have many pictures to choose from after the holidays, but sometimes you want to highlight one great photo. Here are three fast and fun ideas to show you how to do it!

Option 1: Mat photo on white and red paper. Place sticker on bottom corner. Write title on white paper with black Writer and fill in with red lines. Draw holly leaves with green Writer and color in with pencils.

Option 2: Glue photo on white paper. Draw border with gold Opaque marker. Glue on die-cut ornaments. Decorate with stickers, paper, and gold accents. Draw gold lines for hangers. Cut letters from plaid paper and mat on white and red paper. Outline letters with gold. Cut holly berry and leaves from paper and glue on one letter. (Leaves are crimped.)

Option 3: Mat photo on red paper. Pick out colors from photo (the stripes of boy's shirt) and cut small strips of paper to match. Glue diagonally across bottom corner of mat. Make title same as Option 1.

Design from *Creating Keepsakes* magazine

Crimped Wreath

SUPPLIES

- ✤ Fiskars: Paper Edger - Volcano
  Circle Cutter
  Paper Crimper
  Paper Punch
- ✤ Paper Pizazz: Christmas themes
- ✤ Cardstock: Red, green
- ✤ Elmer's Craft Bond Glue Stick

INSTRUCTIONS

Make a textured wreath using a paper crimper. Fold green paper in half and crimp diagonally. Cut leaves in a variety of shapes with Volcano paper edger, having center of leaves along fold. Cut notches in leaves with straight scissors. Arrange in a circle wreath on page and glue down. Cut photos with circle cutter. Trim with paper edger. Cut slightly larger circles for mats. Arrange and glue in place. For berries, punch twenty circles and glue around mat. For bow, cut two 1"x11" strips with paper edger. Crimp strips and fold into shape of bow. Glue on wreath.

Design from Fiskars, Inc.

Angel Wreath

SUPPLIES

- Paper Pizazz: Christmas theme
- Fiskars Paper Edgers: Dragonback, Deckle
- ZIG MS markers: Opaque Writers- White, gold
- Cardstock: White, dark green
- Accu-Cut die-cuts: Small angel small tree
- Elmer's Craft Bond Glue Stick

INSTRUCTIONS

By folding your paper into thirds before inserting it into the die-cut machine, you will get a circle of cuts! When you look closer at this wreath, you will see that there is a circle of angels and a circle of trees. For angels, fold white paper in half. Fold paper into triangular thirds. (See illustration 1.) Place the folded paper on top of the die with the point of paper toward the bottom of the pattern on the die. The folded edges should be just inside the outer edges of the die-cut pattern. Cut the shape and gently unfold the paper. Repeat with green paper for trees.

Cut outside edge of green paper with Deckle paper edger and glue onto white paper. Glue the angels and then the trees on the page. Cut photo in a circle approximately 1/2" smaller than the center of the wreath and mat with white. Cut mat with Dragonback paper edger. Write journaling with white Opaque marker and accent with gold dots.

Design by Julie McGuffee for Accu-Cut

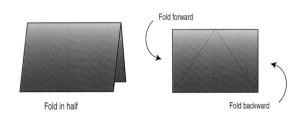

Fold forward

Fold in half

Fold backward

Merry Christmas

SUPPLIES

- Paper Pizazz: Red Plaid paper (Christmas)
- Fiskars Corner Edger: Regal
- ZIG MS marker: Writer - Red, green
- Border Buddy template: #4 - Holiday
- Accu-Cut die-cuts: "Merry Christmas"
- Stickopotamus stickers: Holly
- Elmer's Craft Bond Glue

INSTRUCTIONS

With green Writer, trace holly in two opposite corners. Trace mini Victorian border around page, starting with the top line. Trace bottom line and then trace sides. Trace borders again with red Writer just inside the first line. Doodle bows and dots on outside line with green Writer. Cut out letters and glue on page. Crop photos, trimming corners with Regal corner edger. Mat center photo on plaid paper. Glue photos on page. Add holly stickers. Journal and doodle with both colors of Writer.

Design by Toni Nelson and Beth Reames for EK Success

NEW YEARS EVE

SUPPLIES

+ Fiskars Paper Edger: Mini Pinking
+ ZIG MS markers: Writer - Blue, ocean, pink
    Calligraphy - purple
+ Border Buddy template: #3 - Geo
+ Accu-Cut die-cuts: Party hats, poppers
+ Stickopotamus stickers: Confetti
+ Elmer's Craft Bond Glue Stick

INSTRUCTIONS

Draw Geo border with Writers, using pink for squares, ocean for circles, and blue for triangles. Draw in details for hats, clocks, and party hats. Cut photos in circles and rectangles and mat a few with bright colors. Cut some with Mini Pinking paper edger. Glue photos and die-cuts on page. Write title with ocean and blue Writers. Press on confetti stickers. Journal and add doodles for fun! With broad end of Calligraphy marker, draw purple border edge on page.

Design by Toni Nelson and Beth Reames for EK Success

Easter Morning

SUPPLIES

- ✤ Paper Pizazz: Polka-dot paper (Baby)
- ✤ Fiskars Paper Edger: Pinking
- ✤ ZIG MS markers: Hyacinth Writer
  Black Millennium
  Seashell Opaque Writer
- ✤ Cardstock: Pink, yellow, peach, green, blue, lilac, white
- ✤ Suzy's Zoo stickers: Easter
- ✤ Elmer's Craft Bond Paper Glue

INSTRUCTIONS

Create the excitement of the day with colorful papers, clever cropping of photos, and stickers that interact with what's on the page. Notice the photos that are bumped or silhouetted. The largest rectangle is triple matted. There is a real variety in journaling with lots of information to capture the day for years to come. Polka-dot and white paper are trimmed, then mounted on blue papers for matching borders that tie the two pages together.

Design from *Creating Keepsakes* magazine

4th of July

INSTRUCTIONS

Trace star border around page with blue Opaque Writer. Trace top edge ONLY about 3/4" below top line. Trace stitches and dots with white Opaque Writer just inside first lines. Trace fireworks at random using both Writers. Mat photos on silver paper and glue on page. Glue on star die-cut and press on star stickers. Add journaling.

Design by Toni Nelson for EK Success

Allison 10½ months!

Our Little Pumpkin

our little Pumpkin

SUPPLIES

✢ Paper Pizazz: Green dot paper (Christmas)
    Tan paper
✢ Fiskars Corner Edger: Blossom
✢ ZIG MS markers: Writer, extra fine -
    orange, green
    Opaque Writer, extra fine - orange, green
    Scroll & Brush - green
    Calligraphy - green

✢ Border Buddy template: Jr. - Geometric
    #4 - Holiday
✢ Elmer's Craft Bond Gel

INSTRUCTIONS

Trace pumpkin using #4 template and orange Writer. Trace stem with green Writer and add vines with green Brush marker. Trace scallop border around edge of page, using Jr. Geometric and orange Writer marker. Trace dots using green Writer just inside first line and add hash marks along orange scallops. Crop photos, using

Blossom corner edger and mat on green paper. Write title with green Calligraphy marker on plain paper and mat on green. Dot letters and journal with orange Opaque Writer. Add dots and hash-mark accents.

Design by Toni Nelson and Beth Reames for EK Success

Trim the Tree

SUPPLIES

- Paper Pizazz: Christmas themes Ivory, black, red, yellow, white
- Fiskars: Paper Edger - Scallop Circle Cutter
- ZIG MS markers: Writer - black, red, yellow, orange, blue, green, violet
- X-acto knife
- Elmer's Craft Bond Paper Glue

INSTRUCTIONS

Use Christmas tree lights to make a fun and easy page for the holidays! Write title and draw border with black Writer, using the "Lighten Up" alphabet. Color in bulbs with colored Writers. Cut photos using circle cutter and mat on Christmas papers. Cut mats with Scallop paper edgers. Crop a silhouette photo for bottom left corner, and use an X-acto knife to cut out border so photo will slip in behind it. Add journaling and use bullet tip of red Writer to draw a red border around page.

Design by Carol Snyder for EK Success

Lighten 'Up

LIGHTEN UP ... 🔋 USE BULLET TIP TO WRITE WORD
🔋 USE FINE TIP TO DRAW SQUARES, LINES & BULBS ON LETTER ENDS
🔋 USE FINE TIP TO DRAW "CORD LOOPS & LINES" ON TOP OF LETTERS
🔋 COLOR BULBS AND ADD "SPARKLE" LINES 🔋 REMEMBER...
YOU CAN CREATE "STRING OF LIGHTS" BORDER & ADAPT FOR OTHER HOLIDAYS.

FACE IN HAND

SUPPLIES

✤ Paper Pizazz: Roses (Wedding) white, 2 pink
✤ Fiskars Paper Edgers: Colonial, Scallop, Clouds
✤ Elmer's Craft Bond Gel

INSTRUCTIONS

Sometimes a single photo is all you want on a page for a special effect. However, it would be a good idea to identify the people on the back of the page for future identification. Only the blanket and bracelets are tinted in this black and white photo. There are five mats on the photo, alternating straight and decorative edges.

Design by Debi Boring for *Memory Makers* magazine

A PERFECT TEN

SUPPLIES

✤ Paper Pizazz: Pink gingham
    Bright pink, light pink
✤ Fiskars Paper Edger: Deckle
✤ ZIG MS marker: Black Writer, .5mm
✤ Stickers: Hearts, bows, booties
✤ Elmer's Craft Bond Glue Stick

INSTRUCTIONS

The black and white photos are very dramatic in contrast with the pink papers. This is a ten-minute page that really conveys a strong impact that parents of any age will respond to. Stickers add the final delicate touch to the page.

Design by Kristi Hazelrigg for *Memory Makers* magazine

Baby

SUPPLIES

- ❖ Paper Pizazz: Polka-dot paper (Baby)
- ❖ Fiskars Paper Edger: Dragonback
- ❖ ZIG MS markers: Blue Writer White Opaque Writer, fine tip
- ❖ Accu-Cut die-cuts: "Baby," small baby bottle, stork, bundle, rattle #1
- ❖ Elmer's Craft Bond Paper Glue

INSTRUCTIONS

Cut around polka-dot paper with Dragonback paper edger and glue onto solid paper. Arrange baby die-cuts on a page, overlapping them to create a pleasing flow. Cut out the center of two rattles and use them to frame photos. Crop photos to fit. Arrange silhouetted photos around rattles. Save hearts from handle of rattles and use as accents. Add white dots to "Baby" die-cut and highlights on bottle with the white Opaque Writer. Use blue Writer for lettering and to add stitch lines on hearts.

Design by Julie McGuffee for Accu-Cut

Anna

SUPPLIES

- ❖ Paper Pizazz: Baby block paper (Baby)
  Pastel dot paper
  Yellow paper
- ❖ ZIG MS markers: Fine & Chisel - green, blue jay
- ❖ Accu-Cut die-cuts: Blocks
- ❖ Stickopotamus sticker: It's a Girl
- ❖ Elmer's Craft Bond Paper Glue

INSTRUCTIONS

Tumbling blocks are perfect for including baby's name on a page. Use the "Dot 'n Heart" alphabet on page 65 to write letters on blocks with blue jay Fine & Chisel marker. Cut off two corners of photos diagonally. Double mat photos with plain and patterned papers. Arrange pieces on page and glue down. Add accents and journaling on blocks and mats with green marker. Decorate blocks with stickers.

Design by Carol Snyder and Dale Nicholson for EK Success

A Joyful Note

Make a joyful noise!

OUR LITTLE SOLOIST IS 4 MONTHS OLD!

SUPPLIES

- Paper Pizazz: Black paper
- Fiskars Circle Cutter
- ZIG MS marker: Black Writer, .5mm
- Mrs. Grossman's stickers: Music notes, black design lines
- Elmer's Craft Bond Glue Stick

INSTRUCTIONS

What a fun page! Draw large musical notes on black paper and cut out. Cut photos with circle cutters and glue in center bottom of each note. For musical bar lines, press black stickers horizontally across page, having them evenly spaced. Glue notes on bars and add small sticker notes for accents. Add title and journaling with black Writer.

Design by Debbie Lloyd for Memory Makers magazine

Nana & Mom

SUPPLIES

- Paper Pizazz: Mauve dot paper
- Fiskars Paper Edger: Deckle
- ZIG MS marker: Silver Opaque Writer, extra fine
- Accu-Cut die-cuts: Small banner #3
- White 4" diameter paper doily
- Elmer's Craft Bond Glue Stick

INSTRUCTIONS

Make copies of vintage photos rather than using the originals. The photo in the lower right is a copy of a color photo made on a color copy machine with most of the color taken out, except a little yellow. Check paper doily with pH testing pen. Spray with a de-acidification if necessary. Double mat photos and draw accents on dark paper with silver Opaque marker. Glue two banners on doily and add journaling, using Opaque marker.

Design by Julie McGuffee for Accu-Cut

Molly

SUPPLIES

- Paper Pizazz: Hydrangeas paper (Pretty Papers)
  Laser-cut lace
  Pink, purple (Plain Brights)
- ZIG MS marker: Purple Writer
- Elmer's Craft Bond Glue Stick

INSTRUCTIONS

Florals and lace papers work on baby pages just as well as soft pastels. The lace corners and white photo border come from one sheet of laser-cut paper. The double mat on photo is a combination of a very narrow pink mat on top of a larger purple mat. Don't forget that other items on the page can be matted besides the photos. The lace corners are double matted, too.

Design by Katie Hacker for Hot Off The Press

Ian

SUPPLIES

- ❖ Paper Pizazz: Blue/yellow plaid paper (Light Backgrounds)
    Pastel dot paper
    Blue, yellow paper (Plain Pastels)
    Twinkle, Twinkle (Baby Punch-Outs)
- ❖ Fiskars Paper Edger: Scallop
- ❖ Elmer's Craft Bond Gel

INSTRUCTIONS

Plaid backgrounds make it easy to select coordinating mats for your photos. Remember to take photos of every-day activities as well as special events. Having a variety of shapes when you crop your photos makes for interesting page layouts. You could hand letter Ian's name on blue paper or cut out letters as shown here. The poem and stars lead your eyes through the page.

Design by LeNae Gerig for Hot Off The Press

Crazy Quilt

SUPPLIES

- ❖ Paper Pizazz: 5 Pastel pattern papers (Baby)
- ❖ Fiskars: Rotary Paper Trimmer
    Rotary 45mm Blades - straight, perforating, squiggle
    Self-Healing Mat with Grid
- ❖ Accu-Cut die cuts: "Baby," buggy
- ❖ Elmer's Craft Bond Paper Glue

INSTRUCTIONS

Using a Perforated rotary blade is a quick and easy way to create patchwork pages that actually look like a quilt. With Squiggle blade, cut diagonally (from top right to bottom left and top left to bottom right) through two patterned and two plain 8 1/2"x11" papers. Glue one triangle of each color on a plain whole sheet of paper, leaving 1/8" space between each piece. Glue down. Turn paper over and trim away excess paper on outside edges. To create a "quilt" look, cut perf lines diagonally 1/2" apart with Perforating blade. Crop photo using Squiggle blade and mat on half of one color and half of another. Cut perf lines in die-cuts same as for quilt. Glue photo and die-cuts on page.

Design from Fiskars, Inc.

First Food

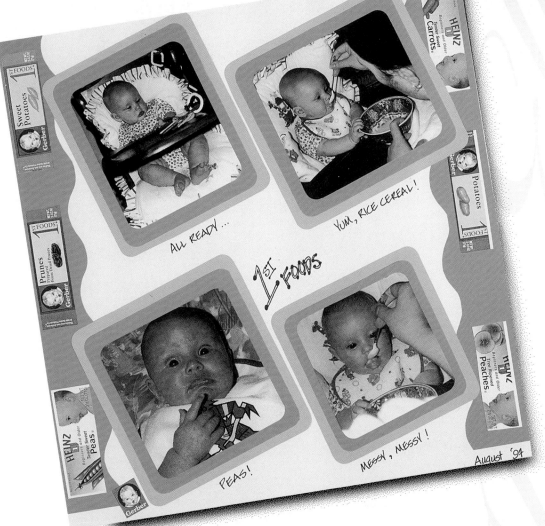

ALL READY ...

YUM, RICE CEREAL!

1ST FOODS

PEAS!

MESSY, MESSY!

August '94

SUPPLIES

- ❖ Paper Pizazz: Gold, turquoise (Solid Brights)
- ❖ Fiskars Corner Edger: Round
- ❖ ZIG MS marker: Black Writer, .5mm
- ❖ Border Buddies template: Original
- ❖ Elmer's Craft Bond Glue

INSTRUCTIONS

Have some fun using baby food labels to decorate a page! Labels were color copied to make the photo safe. Crop photos into squares and rectangles and round corners. Double mat photos on bright papers. Cut strips of paper for side borders, cutting one side with a wavy line. Add your journaling, and the page is done before you know it!

SUPPLIES

- ❖ Paper Pizazz: Yellow, turquoise, red, white (Solid Brights)
- ❖ Fiskars Paper Edgers: Pinking
- ❖ ZIG MS markers: Fine & Chisel - Black, red, orange, violet, evergreen, blue jay, rose
- ❖ Stickopotamus stickers: Transportation
- ❖ Accu-Cut die-cut: Train
- ❖ Elmer's Craft Bond Stick

INSTRUCTIONS

Write letters on white paper with black Fine & Chisel marker, using "Dot 'n Line" alphabet. Draw square block lines with other colors. Add stitching lines with black fine-tip marker. Cut out blocks with a 1/8" border.

Cut a 1 1/4" wide mat for photo. Trim outside edge with Pinking paper edger. Position and glue name blocks and transportation stickers on mat. Cut inside of mat so it is 1" wide, but leave a 1/8" border around stickers and blocks. Add dash and solid lines around border of mat with black marker. Glue photo and mat on turquoise paper. Journal on train die-cut and add stitching lines around the outside edge. Glue on bottom left of mat.

Design by Carol Snyder for Ek Success

Dot & Heart Line

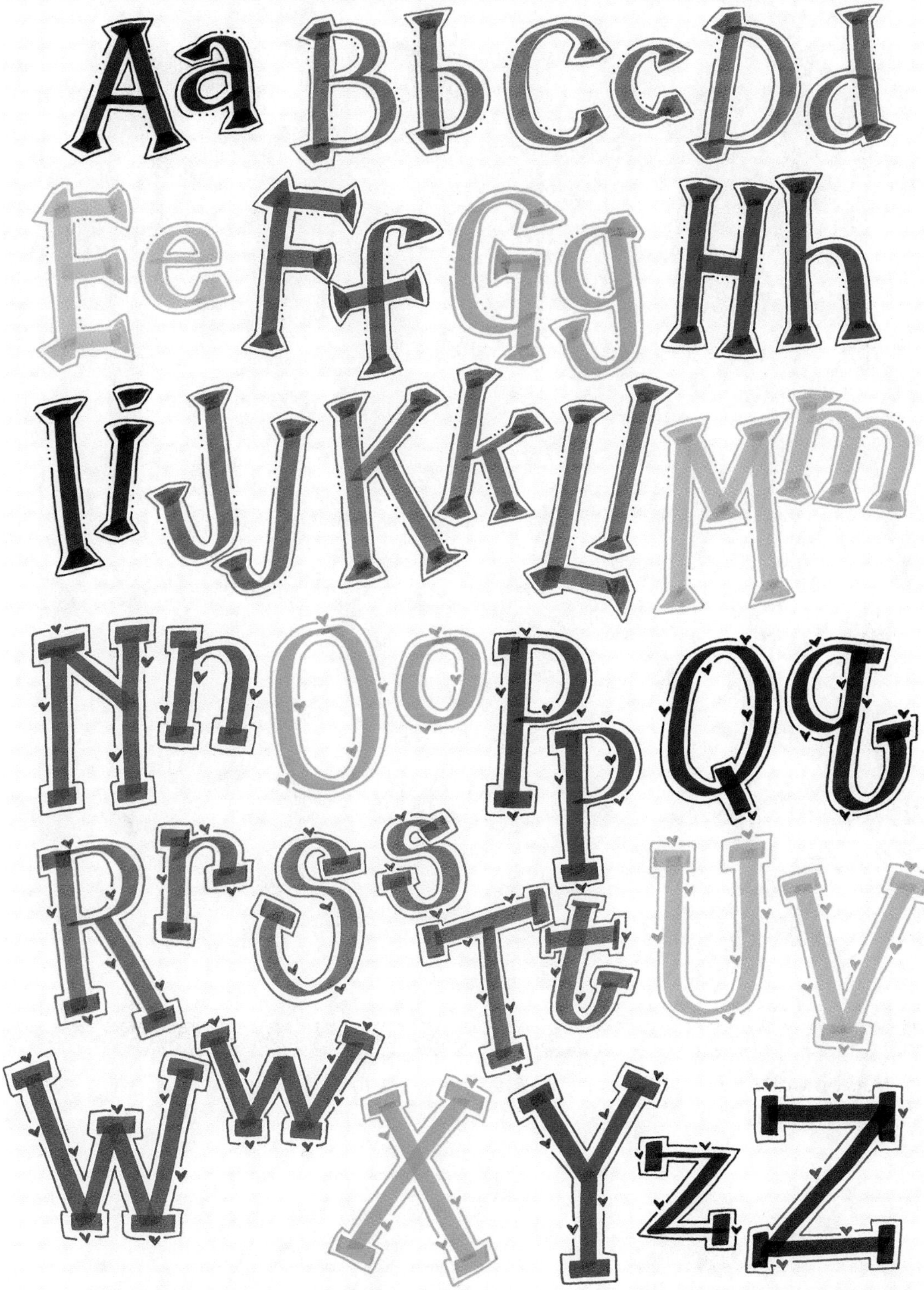

Aa Bb Cc Dd
Ee Ff Gg Hh
Ii Jj Kk Ll Mm
Nn Oo Pp Qq
Rr Ss Tt Uu Vv
Ww Xx Yy Zz

Play Ball

SUPPLIES

- Paper Pizazz: 12" x 12" Grass paper (Pets)
  Baseball paper (Sports)
  Bright red, yellow, blue
  Baseball Punch-Outs
- Fiskars Corner Edger: Contemporary
- ZIG MS marker: White Opaque Writer
- Accu-Cut die-cuts: Letters
- Elmer's Paper Craft Glue Gel

INSTRUCTIONS

Small patterned paper, like the baseball design, is perfect to use for die-cut letters. Imagine this page for any sport! Gluing the letters to rectangles gives them a great accent and personalizes the page using team colors. Punch-out balls add the final touch on one corner of each picture.

Design by LeNae Gerig for Hot Off The Press

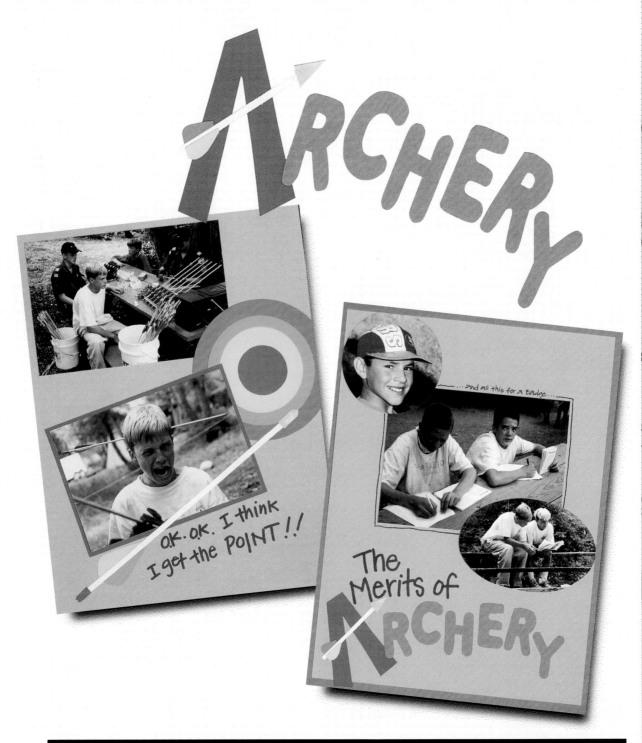

O.K. O.K. I think I get the POINT !!

... and all this for a badge ...

The Merits of ARCHERY

SUPPLIES

- Paper Pizazz: Silver (Metallic)
- Fiskars circle and oval templates
- ZIG MS marker: Black Writer
- Cardstock: Red, yellow, blue, white, green
- Cookie-cutter letters (or stencils)
- Elmer's Craft Bond Glue Stick

INSTRUCTIONS

Have some fun combining appropriate shapes with your sport photos. Crop photos in a variety of shapes and overlap them to guide the eye through the pages. A circle cutter works great for making the target.

Design from *Creating Keepsakes* magazine

Just *KICKIN'* Around

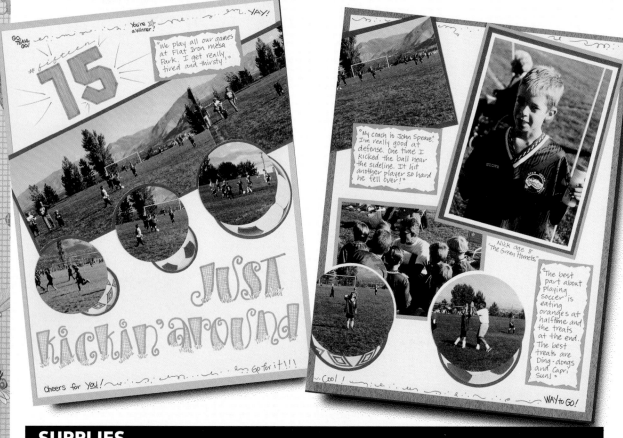

SUPPLIES

- Paper Pizazz: Grass paper (Sports)
  Soccer Ball Punch-Out
- Fiskars: Circle Cutter or circle template
  Paper Edger: Seagull
- ZIG MS markers: Black Millenium
  Dark green, lime green Writer

- Cardstock: White, 2 shades of green
- Suzy's Zoo stickers: Sport
- Elmer's Craft Bond Acid-Free Glue Stick

INSTRUCTIONS

For a green border around each page, trim white cardstock 1/4" on each side and mat on green or grass paper. Gluing two photos together across the spread ties the two pages together. Cut action photos into circles and glue over soccer ball punch-outs. Cut slightly larger circles into bottom of rectangular photos and fit action photos into circles. Draw curly lines with marker and add stickers for the border.

Design from *Creating Keepsakes* magazine

SOCCER Anyone?

SUPPLIES

- Paper Pizazz: Soccer paper (Sports)
- Fiskars: Paper Edger - Dragonback
     Swivel Knife
     Circle Cutter
- ZIG MS marker: Black Millenium
- Elmer's Craft Bond Paper Glue Gel

INSTRUCTIONS

To get interaction between the photos and background paper, cut around hands on photos with a swivel knife. Slip large die-cut soccer balls under the hands. Position photos on decorative paper and lightly mark position with pencil. With swivel knife, partially cut around individual balls that would be under the photo, cutting only to the pencil line. Carefully lift up partially cut soccer balls and slip photos underneath. Glue photos on page and balls in hands.

Design from Fiskars Inc.

Fall COLORS

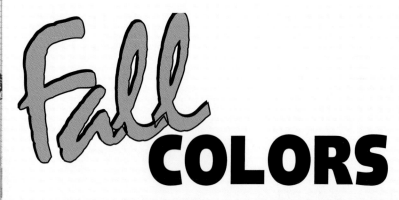

SUPPLIES

- ❖ Paper Pizazz: Frosted leaves paper (Outdoors)
  Orange, burgundy paper (Solid Jewel Tones)
- ❖ Fiskars Paper Edger: Bow tie
- ❖ ZIG MS marker: Black Millennium
- ❖ Accu-Cut die-cut: Leaf
- ❖ Elmer's Craft Bond Glue Stick

INSTRUCTIONS

This is a page that you can do in minutes! Photos are double matted with the second mat cut exactly next to the first one. Be sure to keep your scissors aligned as you cut. A leaf die-cut is glued across the top photo for journaling.

Design by Becky Goughnour for Hot Off The Press

HOOKED *on Fishing*

SUPPLIES

- ❖ Paper Pizzazz: Brown plaid paper (Outdoors)
  Navy and brown (Solid Jewel Tones)
  Barnwood paper (Country)
- ❖ Fiskars Paper Edgers: Cloud, Deckle
- ❖ ZIG MS markers: Fine and Chisel - brown, black
  Opaque Writer - fine-tip silver
- ❖ Stickopotamus: "Fishing" stickers
- ❖ Elmer's Craft Bond Glue Stick

INSTRUCTIONS

Trim 1/4 inch off all sides of tan and cream paper and glue on plaid paper. Use stick lettering and substitute letters with stickers. Add fish hooks to tails of some letters. Cut blue paper for water and barnwood paper for dock. Overlap stickers to create a realistic scene. To make a fish-shaped mat, use an oval template to create the body of the fish and draw half of a triangle for the tail. Draw a fishing line on the pole and attach a bobber.

Design from *Creating Keepsakes* magazine

PICNIC by the Ocean

Picnic by the Ocean

La Jolla, Ca.

Jeff   Brian   Jennie

SUPPLIES

- Paper Pizazz: Grass paper (Pets)
  Clouds paper (Vacation)
  Picnic Ants paper (Outdoors)
  Yellow paper (Plain Brights)
- Fiskars Paper Edger: Pinking

- ZIG MS markers: Scroll & Brush - Red, ocean
- Stickopotamus: "BBQ" stickers
- Accu-Cut die-cuts: Grass, picnic basket
- Elmer's Craft Bond Paper Glue

INSTRUCTIONS

Create a scene with papers and stickers! Have them interact with each other so it looks realistic. The page is simple but very effective because of the choice of colors and papers.

Design from *Creating Keepsakes* magazine

ROCK CLIMBING

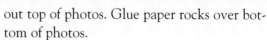

SUPPLIES

- ✤ Paper Pizazz: Beige, blue, tan, clay, bright green paper
- ✤ Fiskars Paper Edger: Peaks
- ✤ ZIG MS markers: Fine & Chisel - brown, spring green
    Writer - black
    Opaque Writer - extra-fine, white
- ✤ Inkworx Air Art Gun
- ✤ Elmer's Craft Bond Paper Glue

INSTRUCTIONS

Use white Opaque Writer and Inkworx gun to create sky effect on solid blue paper. Tear out "rock" shapes from tan and clay paper. Use same white marker and black and brown Fine & Chisel markers with Inkworx gun to create speckled outlines on rocks. Overlap three photos to capture the ascent of the climb, bumping out top of photos. Glue paper rocks over bottom of photos.

Write title on beige paper, using the "Western" alphabet. Use green Fine & Chisel marker for letters and brown for outlines. Cut out each letter with a very thin border and glue on page.

Design by Carol Snyder for EK Success

ROLLERBLADING

SUPPLIES

- ✤ Paper Pizazz: Green, red, orange, blue paper (Plain Brights)
- ✤ Fiskars: Circle Cutter
    Paper Edger - Bubbles
- ✤ ZIG MS markers: Fine & Chisel - black, blue, red
- ✤ Elmer's Craft Bond Glue Stick

INSTRUCTIONS

Capture the action by cutting photos into circles and mounting them on bright papers. Write title with blue Fine & Chisel marker, using "Western" alphabet. Add black broken border.

Design from *Creating Keepsakes* magazine

WESTERN... USE CHISEL TIP & RULER TO FORM
LETTERS -- ADD THICK LETTER ENDINGS
USE FINE TIP TO ADD DOODLES TO LETTERS

A B C D E F G
H I J K L M N
O P Q R S T U V
W W X Y Z

A B C D E F G H I J K L
M N O P Q R S T U V
W X Y Z 1 2 3 4 5 6 7 8 9 0

April Bride

APRIL 26, 1997

SUPPLIES

- Paper Pizazz: Lace paper (Romantic)
  Gold paper (Metallic)
  Ivory, tan paper (Plain Pastels)
  Gold heart charms (Embellishments)
- Fiskars: Paper Edgers - Deckle, Colonial
  Templates - Heart, oval
- ZIG MS marker: Black Millennium
- The Gifted Line stickers: Border, bouquet
- Elmer's Craft Bond Glue

INSTRUCTIONS

Subtle tones of color add to the elegance of lace for a perfect wedding page. Double mat two 3/4" gold paper strips onto ivory and tan papers cut with Colonial paper edger. Glue strips along top and bottom of lace background paper. Press ribbon border stickers down center of each strip. Crop photos in ovals and double mat on ivory and tan papers. Cut a heart from ivory paper and mat on tan. Press bouquet sticker on heart and add journaling. Mat two gold charms on tan and glue on page. It's simple but elegant!

Design by Becky Goughnour for Hot Off the Press

SUPPLIES

- Paper Pizazz: Green marble paper
  (Pretty Papers)
    Antique lace paper
    Green paper (Solid Muted)
- Fiskars Paper Edger: Colonial
- The Gifted Line stickers: Roses
- Elmer's Craft Bond Glue Stick

INSTRUCTIONS

Use colors for mats that will enhance the beauty of the colors within the photo. The plain dark green mat frames the light and dark areas of the photo. The second mat of lace duplicates the lace of the bride's dress. Finally, the green marble mat pulls all of the colors together. Cut triangles for large corner mounts and decorate them with stickers. This page is a classic!

Design by Katie Hacker for Hot Off The Press

Love Doves

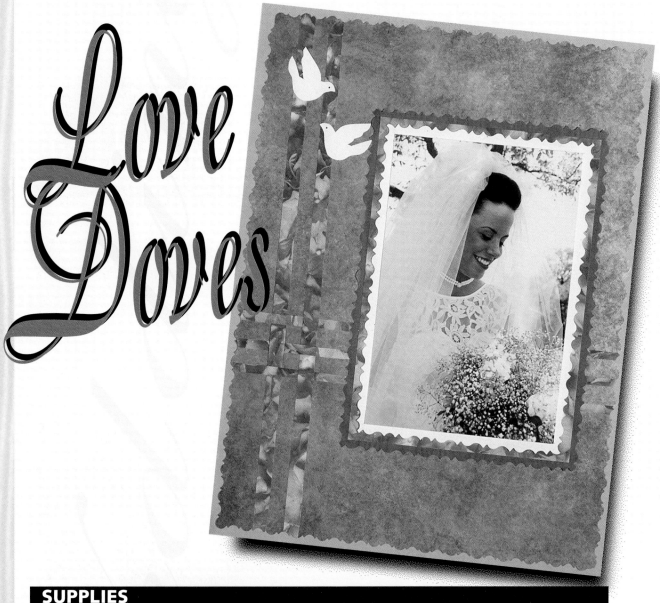

SUPPLIES

- Paper Pizazz: Purple cloud paper (Pretty Papers)
  Azalea paper
  Lavender, purple, white paper (Pastels)
- Fiskars Paper Edgers: Majestic, Victorian
- Accu-Cut die-cuts: Doves
- Elmer's Craft Bond Glue Stick

INSTRUCTIONS

A single photo of the bride should be treated with simple elegance. Triple mat the photo alternating decorative and straight edges. Cut five strips of flowered paper that match the mat and weave them together on one side of photo.

Cut four sides of purple cloud paper with Victorian paper edger and mount on lavender paper. Glue doves on vertical strips.

Design by Julie Stephani for Krause Publications

THE SIGNING

SUPPLIES

- ✤ Paper Pizazz: Pink marble paper (Pretty Paper)
  Rose, lavender, yellow paper
- ✤ Fiskars Paper Edger: Victorian
- ✤ ZIG MS marker: Black Writer
- ✤ Border Buddies: #4
- ✤ Elmer's Craft Bond Glue Gel

INSTRUCTIONS

Capture a special story in pictures. After my future daughter-in-law asked for a Precious Moments figurine for the top of their wedding cake, I had the opportunity to meet Sam Butcher, its creator. I asked him to sign the figurine for them, which he did. The photos tell the story. By cropping photos creatively, you can get quite a few on a page. Single mats and a sillouhette take up less room. Draw a border at the top using a template, and add dot and dashes to give definition to the mats.

Design by Julie Stephani for Krause Publications

BELLS ARE RINGING

SUPPLIES

- ✤ Paper Pizazz: Roses paper (Pretty Papers)
  White, cream, lt. and dark pink, lt. and dark green, yellow
- ✤ Fiskars: Paper Edger - Seagull
  Circle Cutter
- ✤ ZIG MS markers: Fine & Chisel, extra fine
  Gold Opaque Writer
- ✤ Accu-Cut die-cuts: Wedding bells, rings, mini leaves, arch, banner #3, small FR flower
- ✤ Elmer's Craft Bond Glue Gel

INSTRUCTIONS

Look at the special effect you can get by layering die-cuts! Cut four sides of rose paper with Seagull paper edger and glue on cream paper. Glue a white banner on bottom of arch and a cream banner on top of white one. Decorate one side of banner with leaves and other side with flowers and leaves. Crop photo to fit into arch opening and glue on page. Crop photos to fit in center of flower. Glue in place and glue wedding bands on top of flowers. Glue a white bow over cream bow on top of bells. Glue flower and leaves on top of bow. Use Opaque markers to draw dot and line accents.

Design by Julie McGuffee for Accu-Cut

Mini Wedding ALBUM

SUPPLIES

- Paper Pizazz: Pink, green, white paper (Plain Pastels)
- Fiskars Paper Edger: Victorian
- ZIG MS marker: Black Writer
- The Gifted Line stickers: Wedding, cherubs
- Elmer's Craft Bond Glue Stick

INSTRUCTIONS

Mini wedding albums make wonderful gifts, especially when you add your special creative touches to the pages. Photos can be matted in the same way as for larger albums, but you will only have room enough for one photo per page. You may want to keep the pages simple since you will have a whole album to do. Simple mats and sticker accents are a perfect combination; however, you can cut paper the size of the pages to give you more options for decorating. Use banner and border stickers to decorate the first page of the album.

Design by Julie Stephani for Krause Publications

COOL down

SUPPLIES

- Paper Pizazz: Black, white, blue paper
- Fiskars Paper Edgers: Majestic, Leaf
- ZIG MS marker: Black Writer
- Elmer's Craft Bond Paper Glue

INSTRUCTIONS

Capture the fun pictures at weddings as well as the more traditional ones. We had a home reception on a hot summer day for my daughter's wedding. We didn't know the groomsmen had planned for cooler attire when the more formal event was over. The moment was captured and deserved special attention in my album, so I used the tux colors and motifs to carry through onto the page. If you aren't happy with your lettering skills, use the computer to do your journaling. It's neat and foolproof!

Design by Julie Stephani for Krause Publicatons

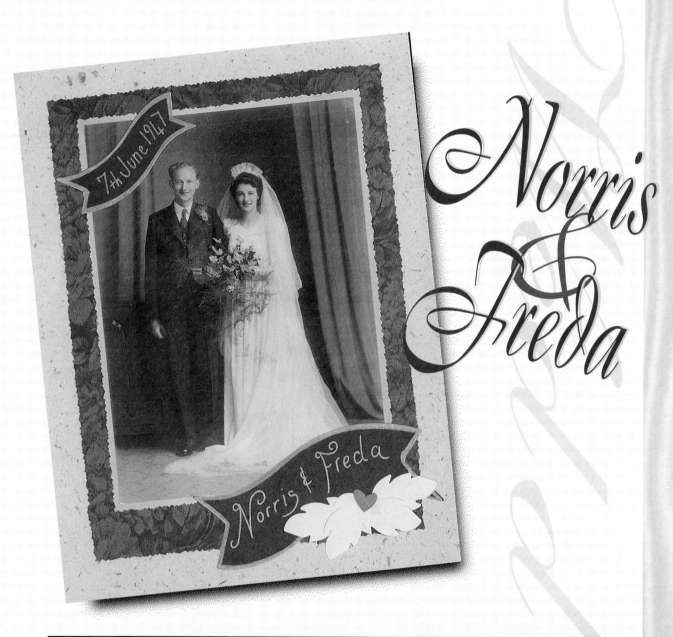

SUPPLIES

- Paper Pizazz: Tapestry paper (Pretty Papers)
  Flecked tan paper (Handmade)
  Peach, burgundy paper
- Fiskars Paper Edger: Deckle
- ZIG MS markers: Gold Opaque
  Writer - extra fine, chisel tip
  Clean Color - pink, green
- Accu-Cut die-cuts: Small and large
  banner #3
- Small paintbrush
- Elmer's Craft Bond Glue

INSTRUCTIONS

Mat photo with narrow peach and wider tapestry mats, cutting them with a Deckle paper edger. Glue on flecked paper. This photo is a color copy of the original and has been gently tinted using the Clean Color markers. A damp paintbrush was drawn across the tip of marker and was used to color in the boutonniere and bouquet in the photo. A large and small banner are used for journaling with the gold Opaque Writer. Four leaves and a gold heart decorate the larger banner.

Design by Julie McGuffee for Accu-Cut

Elaine&Robert

Elaine
and
Robert
DiPalma

5 October 1997

The Wedding Arch

Dancing
to our Song
"All I Ask of You"

Pictures at
Verona Park

Leaving the Church

SUPPLIES

✤ Paper Pizazz: Pink moiré paper
   (Pretty Papers)
   Blue marble paper (Handmade)
   Beige marble paper
   Mauve paper (Solid Muted)

✤ Fiskars: Paper Edger - Ripple
   Corner Edger - Regal
✤ ZIG MS markers: Writer - Black, brown,
   rose, platinum, evergreen
✤ Elmer's Craft Bond Paper Glue

INSTRUCTIONS

Write title on cream rectangle, using Carol's Cursive II alphabet. Cut corners with Regal corner edger. Mat on mauve then purple paper, cutting corners to match. Mat photos on purple and mauve mats, cutting corners with Regal edger or cutting sides with Ripple paper edger. Cut moiré paper into 2" wide ribbon strips and position on pages to connect across the spread. Glue photos and journaling rectangle on top of them. Draw a grapevine border with brown Writer. Add journaling and stitch marks around ribbon. Draw rose and tendril doodles at ribbon ends and corners.

Design by Dale Nicholson and Carol Snyder for EK Success

Carol's Cursive~

to create a more formal lettering style --
use the fine or bullet tip -- slant the letters
and write in cursive or calligraphy.

Aa Bb Cc Dd Ee Ff Gg Hh
Ii Jj Kk Ll Mm Nn Oo Pp
Qq Rr Sss Tt Uu Vv Ww
Xx Yy Zz

Chapter 9: Travel & Scenery

ENGLAND

SUPPLIES

- Paper Pizazz: White, red, blue paper
- ZIG MS markers: 1.2 Writer - Red, blue
- Elmer's Craft Bond Glue

INSTRUCTIONS

Capture the identity of a location through your page layout. Crop photos, bumping some of them. Draw a large letter "E" and cut out from red paper. Cut red strips of paper and blue pieces for flag. Glue pieces on white paper and cut out, leaving a 1/8" border. Arrange letter, flag, photos, and memorabilia on page. Add title.

o n t h e ROAD

SUPPLIES

- ❖ Paper Pizazz: Blue, dark green paper
- ❖ Fiskars Paper Edger: Dragonback
- ❖ ZIG MS markers: Writer - Black, red, green White Opaque Writer, fine tip
- ❖ Accu-Cut die-cuts: 2" marshmallow uppercase alphabet, small car, large banner #3, border die #170
- ❖ Elmer's Craft Bond Glue

INSTRUCTIONS

When you take rolls and rolls of film on a trip, how do you get as many pictures as you can on one of your album pages? Crop them creatively by bumping and silhouetting! This collage of photos includes a map in the background which shows the route taken. (If map is not photo safe, spray it with de-acidification spray.) The background is two-tone paper with white dot accents on the green made with the white Opaque marker. Notice the letters are cut from photos!

Design by Julie McGuffee for Accu-Cut

Spelunking

SUPPLIES

- ✣ Paper Pizazz: Brown plaid paper (Masculine)
- ✣ Cardstock: Beige, maize, oatmeal, olive, 2 brown
- ✣ ZIG MS markers: Black Millennium Opaque Writers - Brown, white
- ✣ Accu-Cut die-cut: Deer
- ✣ Elmer's Craft Bond Glue Gel

INSTRUCTIONS

What if you are too busy having fun on a vacation to snap photos — or your photos just don't turn out? Pick up postcards and brochures on your trip and include them on your scrapbook pages. Sometimes they will have the shot that you never could have taken. A strip of paper glued horizontally across the page serves as a pocket to hold the map and guide. Overlap photos to get more on the page. Write journaling on separate pieces of paper and single mat them.

Design from Creating Keepsakes magazine

Maastricht

SUPPLIES

- ✤ Paper Pizazz: Blue, cream, peach, paper
   Bright pink (Plain Brights)
- ✤ Fiskars Corner Edgers: Blossom, Celestial
- ✤ ZIG MS marker: Pink Writer
- ✤ Elmer's Craft Bond Glue

INSTRUCTIONS

Use corner edgers in a creative way that can actually tie into the theme of the page. Position corner scraps together to make a flower similar to the spring apple blossoms in the photos. Layer cut corners. Add pink dot accents.

Design from Fiskars, Inc.

a day at the BEACH

SUPPLIES

- ✤ Paper Pizazz: Lime, pink, yellow, turquoise
   paper (Solid Brights)
   Tan paper
- ✤ Fiskars Paper Edger: Wave
- ✤ ZIG MS markers: Opaque, extra fine -
   Black, pink, violet, white, harvest
   Opaque writer, fine — Black, orange, yellow
- ✤ Inkworx Air Art Gun
- ✤ Accu-Cut die-cuts: Traveler alphabet
- ✤ Stickopotamus stickers: Beach
- ✤ Elmer's Craft Bond Glue

INSTRUCTIONS

For look of sand, use brown Opaque Writer and Inkworx gun. Crop photos into circles and ovals and mat on bright papers. Silhouette a picture for variety. Write title with brown Opaque Writer and add shadows with harvest Opaque Writer. Add stickers for colorful accents.

Design by Carol Snyder for EK Success

SNOW FORT

SUPPLIES

- Paper Pizazz: Mauve paper (Pearlescent) Turquoise, tan paper
- Fiskars Paper Edgers: Clouds, Mini Scallop
- ZIG MS markers: Opaque Writers, fine & extra fine - Black, white
- Inkworx Air Art Gun
- Memory Pencils, pastel - turquoise
- Stickopotamus stickers: "Snowy Day"
- Elmer's Craft Bond Glue Stick

INSTRUCTIONS

Create the look of snow with white Opaque Writer and Inkworx gun. Mount photos on turquoise and mauve paper, cutting edges with Cloud and Mini Scallop paper edgers. Print letters on separate tan paper, using black Opaque Writer for letters and white Opaque Writer for snow. Use turquoise pencil to create a shaded effect. Cut out letters and mat on mauve rectangle. Add journaling with black and white Opaque Writers. Add stickers to the page for added interest.

Design by Dale Nicholson and Carol Snyder for EK Success

Snow

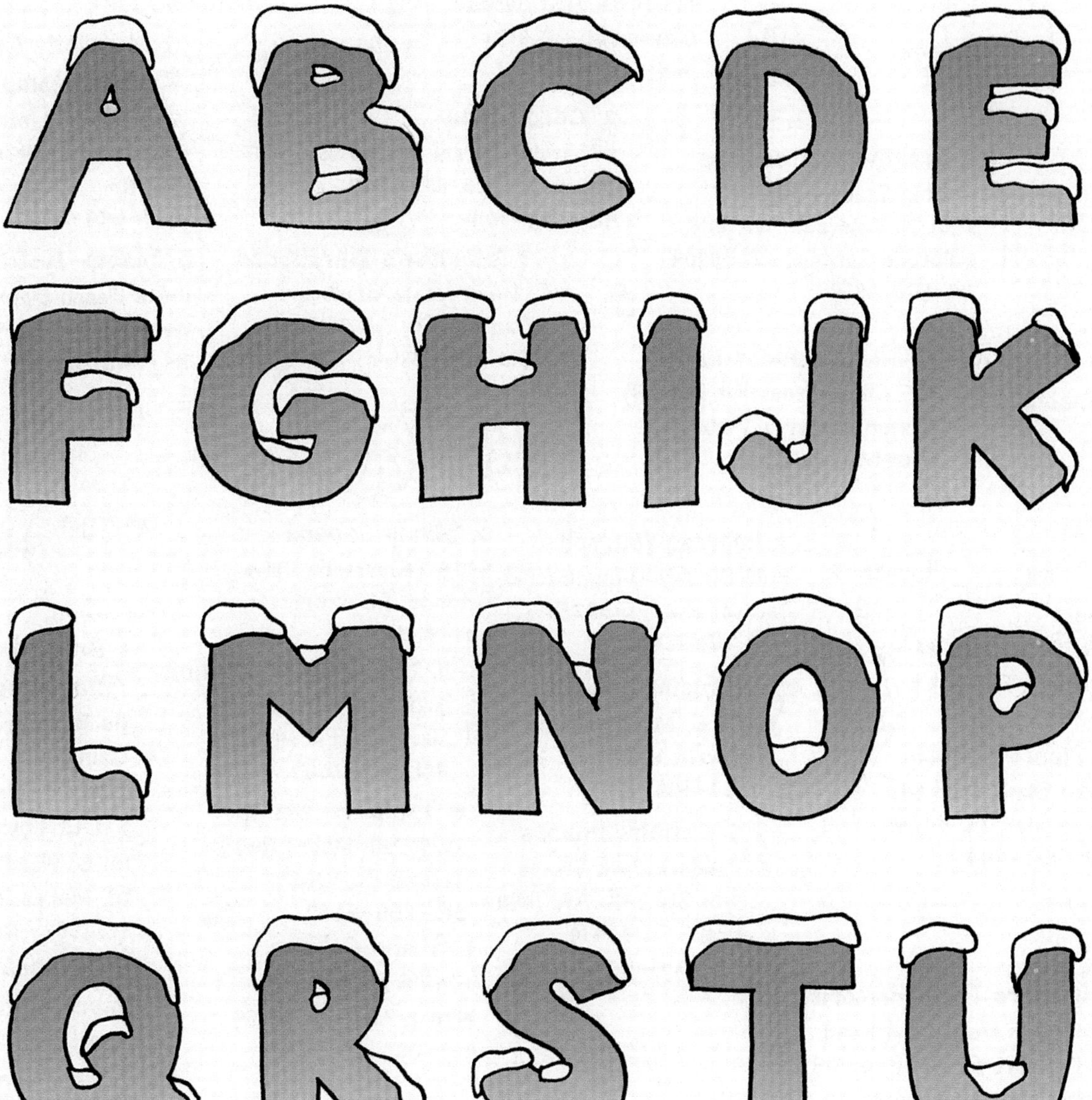

ABCDE
FGHIJK
LMNOP
QRSTU
VWXYZ

Chapter 10: Pets & Animals

CATS
OF THE
NORTH

SUPPLIES

- ✤ Paper Pizazz: Copper striped paper
  (Pearlescent)
  Tan textured paper (Handmade)
  Brown, tan, green paper
- ✤ Fiskars Paper Edgers: Victorian, Peaks,
  Mini Pinking
- ✤ ZIG MS marker: Black Writer
- ✤ Paper punch: Pine tree
- ✤ Elmer's Craft Bond Glue

INSTRUCTIONS

Pick up the highlights in your pet's coloring when you are choosing papers for your pages. Combine close-up photos with further away shots that show them in their natural environment. If you have "pet eye" reflections, use a pen to change the unwanted color to a more natural one. Overlap photos on the page to create a flow in the layout – you will get more pictures on the page, too.

Design by Julie Stephani for Krause Publications

Christmas '97

SUPPLIES

❖ Paper Pizazz: Blue snowflake paper (Christmas)
   Blue, white paper
❖ Fiskars Paper Edger: Dragonback
❖ ZIG MS marker: White Opaque Writer
❖ Accu-Cut die-cut: Small banner
❖ Elmer's Craft Bond Glue Stick

INSTRUCTIONS

Sometimes just allow two great photos to fill the page! Choose papers that compliment the colors and theme of the photos. A simple banner and thin strips of paper glued diagonally across the corners is all that is needed.

Design by Julie Stephani for Krause Publications

Blondie

SUPPLIES

❖ Paper Pizazz: Black, white, 2 blue (Solid Muted)
❖ Fiskars Paper Edger: Peaks
❖ ZIG MS marker: White Opaque Writer
❖ Elmer's Craft Bond Glue Stick

INSTRUCTIONS

Use white mats to bring out your photos on a page. The jagged edge of the circle cut with the Peaks paper edger calls attention to itself, and the silhouetted profile of the horse directs your attention to the same photo. The darker mats on the rectangular photos are offset slightly lower and to the left of the photo for the look of shadowing. For a neat and clean look to your journaling, use your computer and mat the white paper to tie it into the page.

Design by Julie Stephani for Krause Publications

Chew on this

Journaling on layout:
"Snickers" first came to our home after Halloween so we named him in honor of our favorite candy bar. He grew quickly into a giant dog! He is so big that Benji tries to ride on him! He likes to run towards you at top speed until the last second!

Shopping list:
THE NEIGHBORS' SHOES
BAGELS FROM "RICH'S"
DEAD BIRDS
TENNIS BALLS
MY RED LEASH
MY GREEN LEASH
MY BROWN LEASH

CHEW ON THIS...

SNICKERS NET WT 2.07 OZ.

Snickers is a Golden Retriever/Yellow Lab mix. Here's one of the many leashes he chews.

SUPPLIES

- ❖ Paper Pizazz: Paw print paper (Pet)
  Brown paper (Handmade)
  Notebook paper (School Days)
  Cloud Punch-Out
- ❖ Cardstock: White, goldenrod, brown,
  oatmeal, 2 red
- ❖ Fiskars: Paper Edger - Deckle
  Oval template
- ❖ ZIG MS marker: Black Writer
- ❖ Delta Cherished Memories Paper Paint:
  Brown
- ❖ Elmer's Craft Bond Glue Stick

INSTRUCTIONS

Have some fun on your pages and catch the unique personality of your pet. You might even want to try getting a paw print, using acid-free paper paint! Include lots of journaling to tell the stories you can't capture in pictures. If you want to include something on your pages that is not photo safe, spray it with de-acidification spray. Be clever with cropping, silhouetting your pet to hold a shopping list. Allow the corners of photos to go off the pages.

Design from *Creating Keepsakes* magazine

Krista & Papa

Brookfield Zoo

Alex

Brookfield Zoo

SUPPLIES

❖ Paper Pizazz: Yellow, green, blue, red (Plain Brights)
❖ Fiskars Paper Edgers: Stamp, Leaf
❖ ZIG MS marker: Black Writer
❖ Mrs. Grossman's sticker: Bird
❖ Elmer's Craft Bond Glue Stick

INSTRUCTIONS

Next time you go to the zoo to take photos of the animals, be sure to turn your camera towards the people who are enjoying the sights. The combination of photos on your album pages will capture the adventure of the day. It takes patience to keep your camera focused on the animals to catch them at a good angle, but it will be worth your time. Don't be afraid to use bright colors that balance with each other. Notice how the bird sticker ties two photos together.

Design by Julie stephani for Krause Publications

Hip Hop

SUPPLIES

- Paper Pizazz: Yellow, green, purple, pink (Plain Brights)
- Fiskars Paper Edger: Deckle
- ZIG MS markers: Black Writer
  Opaque Writer - White, pink, orange
- Accu-Cut die-cuts: Letters, eggs, grass
- Elmer's Craft Bond Glue Stick

INSTRUCTIONS

Capture the action of the moment by taking photos in close sequence and then overlapping them on your album page. Your eyes begin in the top left corner, travel down the right, and end with the largest photo which is your focal point. You can emphasize the main interest photo by using brighter or additional mats. The black stitch lines are important in establishing definition among all of the bright colors. Add accents to the eggs and letters with Opaque Writers.

Design by Julie Stephani for Krause Publications

Where's Charlie?

SUPPLIES

- Paper Pizazz: Yellow, orange, gold (Plain Brights)
- Fiskars: Corner Edger - Blossom
  Pet Stencil
- ZIG MS marker: Black Writer
- Elmer's Craft Bond Glue

INSTRUCTIONS

Get creative with a pet paw stencil! Trim corners of photo and mats with the Blossom corner edger. Mat on orange and then yellow paper, having mat wide enough for paw prints. Notice how flower is bumped out of photo and has the orange mat around it. Stencil paw print around mat and going off the top and bottom of page.

Design from Fiskars, Inc.

Cat & Mouse

* Delta Cherished Memories:
  Cat stencil
  Stencil adhesive dots
  Stencil sponges
* Acid-free paper paints: Mint kiss, yellow
  charm, summer sky blue, dark butter
  scotch, dark rose, breezy lilac, fresh green,
  pink kiss, black
* 14" square frame
* 1/2" flat paintbrush
* Elmer's Craft Bond Glue

INSTRUCTIONS

For best results, stencil with an up and down "pouncing" motion. Base coat frame and inner mat with pink paint.

All mice are stenciled with black paint. Stencil mouse around edge of inner mat. Stencil mouse on outer mat and frame as shown in photo. Cat and frame in bottom left corner is stenciled with mint kiss, shaded lightly with black. Cat in bottom right corner has body stenciled with pink kiss, shaded lightly with black. The ears, paws, and tail are black highlighted with pink. The cat above the center photo is stenciled with butterscotch, shaded lightly with black. Cat in top left corner is stenciled with sky blue but has black ears. Cat in upper right corner is stenciled with lilac but has black ears and paws. Cut photo to fit in stencil in bottom left corner. Insert second photo behind center mat.

Design by Gail Armstrong for Delta Technical Coatings, Inc.

puppy love

SUPPLIES

- ✤ Paper Pizazz: Dog bones paper (Pets)
    Lime, peach, blue, gold, gray
- ✤ Fiskars: Paper Edgers - Scallop, Volcano
    Corner Edger - Art Deco
- ✤ ZIG MS markers: Gray Calligraphy
    Black Millennium, .01
- ✤ Stickopotamus stickers: Dog accessories
- ✤ Elmer's Craft Bond Glue

INSTRUCTIONS

Crop photos into a variety of shapes, including bumping and silhouetting if appropriate. Double or triple mat photos in colors to match background paper. Cut a rectangle and a square for journaling and mat them. Use "Tall and Skinny" alphabet for lettering with the gray Calligraphy marker. Use black Millennium marker to add dash lines to letters and mats. Press on stickers for accents.

Design by Carol Snyder for EK Success

CAT naps

SUPPLIES

- ✤ Paper Pizazz: Paw prints paper (Pets)
    Tan, blue, dark green paper
- ✤ ZIG MS markers: Calligraphy - black, red, violet,
    evergreen
    Black Millennium, .01
- ✤ Stickopotamus stickers: Cat accessories
- ✤ Elmer's Craft Bond Glue

INSTRUCTIONS

Crop photos creatively to include more on the page. Notice that it is better to cut slightly outside the cat in order to get the fur outline. Cut rectangles for journaling. Use the "Tall & Skinny" alphabet for journaling in a variety of colored Calligraphy markers. Press stickers on page for accents. Use black Millennium marker to outline stickers and draw squiggle and hash lines around cropped photos.

Design by Dale Nicholson and Carol Snyder for EK Success

Tall & Skinny

ABCD abcd EFGH efgh IJK
i j k LMNO lmno PQRS pqrs
T UVW tuvw XYZ xyz

Try printing your letters
TALL & SKINNY.
Put long stems on your letters!
Remember... you can create all letters with the broad & narrow tips!

Aa Bb Cc Dd Ee
Ff Gg Hh Ii Jj Kk Ll
Mm Nn Oo Pp Qq Rr
Ss Tt Uu Vv Ww Xy Zz

Print Letters. Add triangles, straight lines or double lines to the ends of the letters. You can shadow too!

Chapter 11: Kids & School

4th Grade

SUPPLIES

- ✤ Paper Pizazz: School supplies paper (School Days)
  Green, red, yellow, orange paper
  Number, pencil Punch-Outs
- ✤ Fiskars Paper Edgers: Scallop, Mini Pinking
- ✤ ZIG MS marker: Black Writer
- ✤ Suzy's Zoo sticker
- ✤ Mrs. Grossman's stickers: Cat, apple, bus, alphabet border
- ✤ Accu-Cut die-cut: Apple
- ✤ Elmer's Craft Bond Glue

INSTRUCTIONS

Make a school album to collect each year's photos and memories from kindergarten to graduation. For each year, include specific information and class pictures. Make one page into a large pocket to hold report cards, ribbons, awards, etc. Decorate the pages with stickers and die-cuts that reflect the child's special interests.

Albums can be as simple as two pages for each grade — or the number of pages can be expanded to include photos and memorabilia from additional activities. The album would make a wonderful graduation gift at the end of the child's senior year of high school.

Design by Julie Stephani for Krause Publications

Ari

SUPPLIES

- ❖ Paper Pizazz: Raindrop paper (Child's Play)
    Blue, yellow paper (Plain Brights)
    Raindrop Punch-Outs
- ❖ Fiskars Paper Edger: Beat
- ❖ ZIG MS marker: Black Millennium
- ❖ Accu-Cut die-cuts: Marshmallow alphabet
- ❖ Elmer's Craft Bond Glue

INSTRUCTIONS

The yellow of Ari's slicker is duplicated in the die-cut letters and mats around his photos. The large raindrops echo the raindrop patterned paper and add to the rainy day theme. Mat letters, photos, and the journaling oval to match each other. The page is very effective because the colors are so well coordinated.

Design by Becky Goughnour for Hot Off The Press

Rub-A-Dub-Dub

SUPPLIES

- ❖ Paper Pizazz: Bubble paper (Childhood)
    Blue, white paper
- ❖ Fiskars: Paper Edger - Jigsaw
    Circle cutter
- ❖ ZIG MS marker: Black Writer
- ❖ Elmer's Craft Bond Glue Stick

INSTRUCTIONS

Sometimes journaling can pull photos together on a page by making a connection between them. I wanted to do a page of my grandkids in the bathtub, but Jacob wasn't in the picture. I just made up a little poem so I could include him, too. It worked, and the page went together in minutes! (Bubbles are great for journaling.)

Design by Julie Stephani for Krause Publications

OFF TO SCHOOL

SUPPLIES

✤ Paper Pizazz: Paint Splash paper (School Days)
  Green, gold, blue, red, brown paper
  "Off to School", bus Cut Outs
✤ ZIG MS markers: Black Writer
  Red Calligraphy Writer
✤ Accu-Cut die-cuts: 2" Marshmallow alphabet, large
  school frame
✤ Elmer's Craft Bond Glue

INSTRUCTIONS

When you use die-cuts and cut-out shapes, pages go together in a jiffy! Cut 1/2" from one short and one long side of pattern paper and glue onto green paper.

Silhouette one photo and mat on gold paper. Draw bricks on schoolhouse with red

Calligraphy marker. Place photo in schoolhouse frame. Arrange and glue pieces on page. Add lines, squiggles and dots on schoolhouse, letters, and around borders.

Design by Julie McGuffee for Accu-Cut

SCHOOL DAYS

SUPPLIES

✤ Paper Pizazz: Graduation paper (School Days)
  Red, gold, 3 green
  Diploma Punch-Out
✤ Fiskars Paper Edger: Dragonback
✤ Zig MS marker: Black Writer
✤ Accu-Cut die-cuts: Small school picture frame, grass border
✤ Elmer's Craft Bond Glue Stick

INSTRUCTIONS

Cut 1/2" from top and both long sides of pattern paper, using Dragonback paper edger. Glue onto red paper. Die-cut three shades of green grass and glue them together, having them staggered. Cut bottom edges even. Cut an oval for journaling and mat with red. Crop a photo in silhouette.

To make the circle of schoolhouses, fold red paper into thirds before inserting it into the die-cut machine.(See illustration 1.) Place the folded paper on top of the die with the point of paper toward the bottom of the pattern on the die. The folded edges should be just inside the outer edges of the die-cut pattern. Cut the shape and gently unfold the paper.

Mark frame openings on the back of photos and cut photos 1/4" larger than the openings. Arrange and glue everything on the page.

Design by Julie McGuffee for Accu-Cut

❶ Fold in half

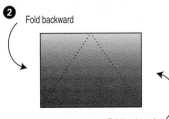

❷ Fold backward

Fold backward

Hannah COLORS

SUPPLIES

❖ Paper Pizazz: Red dotted paper (Ho Ho Ho!)
  Crayon paper (School Days)
  Crayons Punch-Outs
  Blue, red, green, yellow, purple paper
  (Plain Brights)

❖ Fiskars Paper Edger: Clouds
❖ ZIG MS marker: ; Black Writer
❖ Elmer's Craft Bond Glue

INSTRUCTIONS

This double-page spread uses brightly pattern papers to echo the enthusiasm Hannah shows as she creates her personal art! The center oval of the dotted paper becomes the middle of the crayon paper and vice versa. Simple plain corners connect the two pages. The photo mats of plain papers have black dots along the scallops. The crayons, crayon box, and child's drawing have a white border to separate them from the pattern papers. Primary colors are perfect for kids' pages!

Design by LeNae Gerig for Hot Off The Press

First Day

SUPPLIES

+ Paper Pizazz: Yellow lined paper (School Days)
    Red dotted paper (Ho Ho Ho!)
    Red, blue paper
+ Fiskars: Paper Edgers - Pinking, Zipper
    Corner Edger - Art Deco
+ ZIG MS Markers: Writer - Black, red
    Black Millennium, .01
+ Stickopotamus stickers: Push pins
+ Elmer's Craft Bond Glue Stick

INSTRUCTIONS

Print title on white paper with blue Writer, using "Dot" alphabet. Add shadow with red Writer. Cut rectangle with Zipper paper edger and mount on red dotted paper. Add dash lines with black Millennium marker. Print date on small rectangle and mat on blue paper. Crop photos and cut corners with Art Deco corner edger. Mat pictures on red or blue papers and cut corners in same way. Arrange and glue pieces on yellow lined paper. Print journaling with red and blue Writers. Add push-pin stickers.

Design by Carol Snyder for EK Success

Report Cards

SUPPLIES

+ Paper Pizazz: Red/yellow plaid paper (School Days)
    Yellow, red paper
+ Fiskars Paper Edger: Zipper
+ ZIG MS markers: Writer - Red, Black, blue
    Black Millennium, .01
+ Border Buddy template: #3 - Geo
+ Stickopotamus stickers: Classroom
+ Elmer's Craft Bond Glue

INSTRUCTIONS

Cut red and yellow papers in half to form four 5 1/2"x8 1/2" pieces. Trim all four sides of one yellow piece with Zipper paper edgers. Glue on one red piece for front of pocket. For borders, cut remaining yellow piece into three 1/2"x8 1/2" strips. Trim one long side of each strip with paper edger. Glue one strip along top of plaid paper and other two down the sides. Glue front of pocket on bottom half of plaid paper, gluing close to the edges on three sides ONLY, leaving top open.

Using template, draw border around all four sides of pocket with black Writer. Use fine tip to add dash lines on outside of border. Print journaling on pocket with blue and red Writers, using the "Dot" alphabet. Add dash line shadows in contrast color. Add sticker accents and glue photo in top left corner.

Design by Carol Snyder for EK Success

Dot

DOT LETTERING ·····..·····
Aa Bb Cc Dd Ee Ff Gg Hh Ii Jj Kk Ll
Mm Nn Oo Pp Qq Rr Ss Tt Uu Vv
Ww Xx Yy Zz

USING FINE TIP, WRITE LETTERS ·· USE BULLET TIP TO HIT ENDS OF EACH LETTER
QUICK, easy and FUN DOT LETTERS!

Aa Bb Cc Dd Ee Ff Gg Hh Ii
Jj Kk Ll Mm Nn Oo Pp Qq Rr
Ss Tt Uu Vv Ww Xx Yy Zz

LARGER DOT LETTERING -- USE BULLET TIP TO WRITE LETTERS
AND TO DRAW DOTS ON WITH a CIRCULAR MOTION.

single line letters -- REMEMBER
YOU CAN USE THE FINE & BULLET
TIPS IN DIFFERENT COMBINATIONS
WRITE WITH THE FINE TIP--LINE WITH FINE OR BULLET
WRITE WITH THE BULLET TIP--LINE WITH THE BULLET OR FINE
aBCD -- EFGH -- IJKL -- MNOP

Chapter 12:
Seasons

Spring Trees

SUPPLIES

✤ Paper Pizazz: Lime, yellow paper (Plain Brights)
  Purple, brown (Solid Muted)
✤ Fiskars: Paper Edger - Victorian
  Corner Edger - Summit
✤ ZIG MS marker: Black Writer
✤ Elmer's Craft Bond Glue Stick

INSTRUCTIONS

Keep mats simple when you want to show off the details of the photos. Each individual mat was chosen to highlight a color in a photo. Add dot and line accents on mats with black Writer.

Design by Julie Stephani for
Krause Publications

Summer Fields

SUPPLIES

✤ Paper Pizazz: Gold, fuchsia, white
  (Plain Brights)
✤ Fiskars Paper Edgers: Peaks, Seagull

✤ ZIG MS markers: Black Writer
✤ Mrs. Grossman's stickers: Snakes
✤ Elmer's Craft Bond Glue Sticks

INSTRUCTIONS

Purple, white, and gold fields full of flowers are showcased by the same colored mats. Narrow strips of paper connect some of the photos. These pages underline the importance of journaling. If you weren't told, you wouldn't know that after spending a day frolicking in the fields of flowers, that night they found out the fields were full of rattlesnakes!

Design by Julie Stephani for Krause Publications

UP NORTH

SUPPLIES

- Paper Pizazz: Brown plaid paper (Outdoors) Brown, black, 2 green papers
- Fiskars Paper Edger: Leaf
- ZIG MS marker: Black Writer
- Elmer's Craft Bond Glue

INSTRUCTIONS

Dark green and brown mats bring out the colors of the fall woods and fields. The single mats add simple lines to the page. Only one double-matted corner is used in the top right corner to balance with the plaid strips of paper running behind the photos. Sometimes less is more.

Design by Julie Stephani for Krause Publications

Pumpkin Pocket

SUPPLIES

- Paper Pizazz: Tan, green, orange, brown, black (Plain Brights)
- Fiskars: Paper Edgers - Dragonback, Pinking, Ripple, Zipper, Notch, Clouds
  Paper Punch - Heart
  Paper Crimper
- ZIG MS marker: Green Writer
- Elmer's Craft Bond Glue

INSTRUCTIONS

Cut out five different shaped pumpkins with five different paper edgers. Fold each pumpkin in a fan fold and roll through crimper. Unfold pumpkins and mat on black paper trimmed with Pinking paper edger. Crop and glue photos on two pumpkins. Overlap and glue pumpkins on the tan paper, leaving tops open to form a pocket for your favorite pumpkin recipe. Cut small odd shapes for leaves; fold in half and crimp. Glue leaves on tops of some pumpkins. Cut black paper and glue on for the faces. For pumpkin seeds, punch twelve hearts from light brown paper and cut in half. Glue around edges of page. Add squiggle lines with green Writer. Add journaling.

Design from Fiskars, Inc.

PICK of the PATCH

The Pick of the Patch

SUPPLIES

- Paper Pizazz: Barnwood paper (Country) Orange, rust, squash, maize, hunter green, oatmeal
- White cardstock
- Fiskars Circle Cutter
- ZIG MS marker: Brown Writer
- Clear plastic memorabilia envelop, 3L
- Elmer's Craft Bond Glue

INSTRUCTIONS

What a great combination of photos, creative cropping and matting, and the added dimension of raffia and pumpkin seeds. These pages really pull the elements together to make you feel like you are there. By including items from nature and coordinating background colors, you can preserve the rich beauty of the fall season.

Design from *Creating Keepsakes* magazine

TEXAS snow

SUPPLIES

- ❖ Paper Pizazz: Blue snowflake paper (Christmas)
     White, blue paper
- ❖ Fiskars Paper Edger: Dragonback
- ❖ ZIG MS markers: Black Writer
     White Opaque Writer
- ❖ Accu-Cut die-cuts: Small snowflake #1,
     small heart #2, small banner #3
- ❖ Elmer's Craft Bond Glue

INSTRUCTIONS

Trim all sides of snowflake paper 1/2" with Dragonback paper edger. Glue onto white paper. Cut one photo in a heart and silhouette the other. Mat heart photo on blue paper. Cut one white and one blue banner. Glue blue banner slightly below white one. Arrange and glue pieces on the page along with two snowflake die-cuts. Journal with black Writer and make white dots around heart with white Opaque Writer.

Design by Julie McGuffee for Accu-Cut

WINTER on holly hedge

SUPPLIES

- ❖ Paper Pizazz: Snowflake paper (Christmas)
     Blue pattern paper (Light Great)
     Snowflake Punch-Out
- ❖ Fiskars Paper Edger: Deckle
- ❖ ZIG MS marker: Blue Writer
- ❖ Elmer's Craft Bond Glue

INSTRUCTIONS

Each of three photos is triple matted, beginning with a pattern paper that resembles handmade. The photos are cropped in different shapes to add interest to the page. A rectangle is cut for journaling and is also triple matted.

Design by Katie Hacker for Hot Off The Press

Winter Wonderland

SUPPLIES

❖ Paper Pizazz: Purple textured paper
  (Pretty Papers)
  Plaid paper (Light Great Backgrounds)
  Blue, white, gray, purple paper
❖ Fiskars: Paper Edgers - Seagull, Deckle
  Circle & oval templates
❖ ZIG MS markers: Opaque Writers - White,
  purple
  Millennium Writer - Purple
❖ The Gifted Line stickers: Winter, sleigh ride
❖ Elmer's Craft Bond Glue

INSTRUCTIONS

Some pages are worth taking the extra time to capture the season and event. To create the background on the left page, tear textured cardstock in a snow-pile pattern. Trim colored paper with Deckle paper edger and place behind the snow. Press on stickers to create a winter scene. A sticker frame is used for the large photo on the right page. Cut a large plaid scarf to fit the silhouetted boy in the bottom right corner. Outline title with the purple Writer and fill in with the lilac Opaque Writer. Use a white Opaque Writer to add snow. Journal with the purple Millennium Writer.

Design from *Creating Keepsakes* magazine

Springtime

SUPPLIES

- Paper Pizazz: Orange, peach, beige, 2 greens
- Fiskars Corner Edger: Provincial
- ZIG MS markers: Scroll & Brush - Orange, yellow, green
    Writer - Orange, green
- Border Buddy template: #3 Geo
- Stickopotamus stickers: Daffodils
- X-acto knife
- Elmer's Craft Bond Glue Stick

INSTRUCTIONS

Trim corners of photos with Provincial corner edger. Double mat photos, cutting same corners. Using a template, trace border edge around paper with scroll tip of green Scroll & Brush marker. Add lines for picot ribbon edges with brush tip. Add color to ribbon with yellow marker. Write title using scroll tip of orange Scroll & Brush marker, using the "Scroll & Brush" alphabet. Add ribbon picot lines and fill in with yellow brush tip. Glue photos on page, cutting around tail of "g" with knife to insert photo underneath. Press daffodils along borders, making small slits just above border on bottom of page to insert the flower stems. Print names and journaling. Add doodle dots and leaves.

Design by Carol Snyder for EK Success

Aa Bb Cc Dd
Ee Ff Gg Hh Ii
Jj Kk Ll Mm
Mm Nn Oo Pp
Qq Rr Ss Tt
Uu Vv Ww
Xx Yy Zz

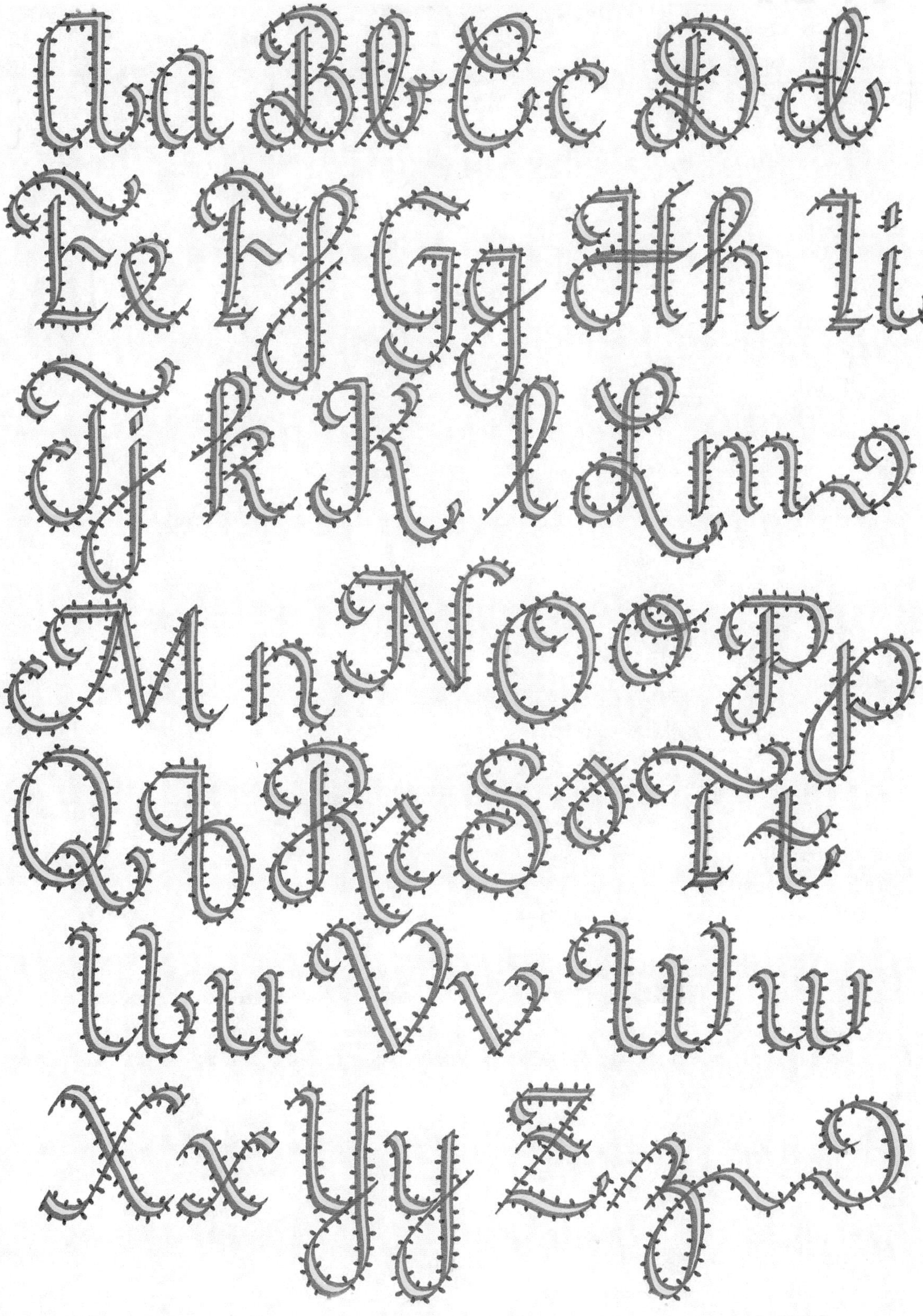

CHRISTMAS FRAME

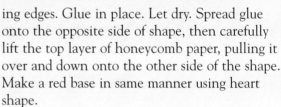

SUPPLIES

- Paper Pizazz: Red Polka-Dot paper (Christmas) Red, green paper
- Red Cardstock
- Red and Green Honeycomb Paper
- ZIG MS markers: Writers - Black, green, red Chisel Tip Opaque Writer - Red, white Green Calligraphy Marker
- Accu-Cut die-cuts: Train #4, small heart #3, mini stars, small oval, confetti
- ZIG Ready-To-Make Large Frame
- Stylus
- Elmer's Craft Bond Glue

INSTRUCTIONS

To paint inside and outer edges of frame green with the Calligraphy marker, lay the center of the wide calligraphy tip on edge frame. With even pressure, slowly pull the nib along edge. Pressure will determine width of the line. Add a double dot and squiggle border along green edge. Cut the train shape from green and red polka-dot paper. Glue red on the green, having it offset. Cut two yellow shades of stars and glue together, having them offset.

For honeycomb shapes, cut a tree from green and a heart from red paper. For tree, cut a rectangle of green honeycomb paper a little longer than the length of the tree pattern and approximately 3" wide. (Note: lines on the honeycomb paper should always be horizontal.) Place honeycomb paper on top of plain paper with edge of the honeycomb paper on center line of the pattern. The honeycomb will be only half of a pattern. Cut the shape then carefully remove paper from the die. Glue honeycomb shape on one side of the full Christmas tree shape, align-

ing edges. Glue in place. Let dry. Spread glue onto the opposite side of shape, then carefully lift the top layer of honeycomb paper, pulling it over and down onto the other side of the shape. Make a red base in same manner using heart shape.

Glue tree and heart on one side of frame. Outline right side of the star with large tip of the red Writer. Outline right side of clouds and train with black Writer. Add black dash lines on train. Use white chisel tip Opaque marker for lettering on clouds. Add accents with the black fine-tip Writer. Write "Christmas" with red Opaque marker and outline with green Writer.

For center mat, cut a rectangle from red cardstock and cut an oval from the center. To emboss mat, use the heart pattern on smoke stack of train and a stylus. Place photo behind mat and place in frame.

Design by Julie McGuffee for Accu-Cut

Picture Ornament

SUPPLIES

- Paper Pizazz: Red plaid paper (School Days)
    Red, green, brown paper
- ZIG MS marker: Black writer
- Accu-Cut die-cuts: Apple, schoolhouse
- Mrs. Grossman's stickers: Bus, child
- Red 1/8" wide ribbon, 8 inches
- Elmer's Craft Bond Glue

INSTRUCTIONS

Use die-cuts to make a quick gift. Trace opening of frame onto back of photo. Cut photo 1/14" larger than opening. Glue in place. Press stickers along base of schoolhouse. Overlap and glue frame onto apple. Trace leaf on green and stem on brown paper and cut out. Glue pieces on die-cut. For hanger, glue ribbon ends together, forming a loop. Glue ends on center back of die-cuts.

Design by Julie Stephani for Krause Publicatons

Little Gladys

SUPPLIES

- Paper Pizazz: Pink Roses paper (Wedding)
    Pink Moiré paper
    Rose, peach, cream paper
- Fiskars: Paper Edgers - Scallop, Ripple, Clouds, Seagull
    Corner Edgers - Nostalgia
    Paper Punch - Heart
    Transparent Photo Corner
- Elmer's Craft Bond Glue

INSTRUCTIONS

Give a vintage photo as a gift. Mount photo on roses paper with photo corners. Trim mat with Scallop paper edger. Cut corners of roses and rose paper with Nostalgia corner edger and sides with Ripple paper edger. Glue matted photo onto center of moiré paper. With paper edgers, cut various widths of paper strips from different papers. To create "pearl" looking strip, cut one side of strip with Scallop and simply "flip" scissors and cut in opposing direction. Glue diagonally across paper as shown. Punch out hearts and glue in place.

Design from Fiskars Inc.

Baby FRAME

SUPPLIES

- Paper Pizazz: Bubbles paper (Baby)
    It's a Boy!
- ZIG MS markers: Blue Chisel Tip
    White fine-tip Opaque Writer
- ZIG¨ Ready-To-Make Classic Frame
- Cardstock - Pale Blue, Medium Blue
    and White
- White Honeycomb Paper
- Accu-Cut die-cuts: Small baby carriage,
    small circle, small banner #3, stork and
    bundle
- Stylus
- Matte Decoupage Finish
- Paintbrush
- Elmer's Craft Bond Glue

INSTRUCTIONS

Shapes cut with the die cut machine result in two pieces: a die cut shape and a template. The template can also be used as a stencil and a mat to frame a photograph.

Trace around frame onto Bubbles paper. Cut out and glue to front of the frame. Paint with two coats of decoupage finish. Let dry. Color the inside and outside edges of the frame, using blue Chisel Tip marker. Cut a stork and bundle, one small circle, and two smaller circles (use baby carriage wheels as a pattern) from white paper. Cut the baby carriage from "It's a Boy" paper.

Cut three squares of honeycomb paper a little larger than the paper circles. (Note: the lines on the honeycomb paper should always be horizontal.) Place honeycomb paper on top of half of the die pattern. The honeycomb will be only half of the circle. Cut the shape and carefully remove the honeycomb paper from the die. Glue on half of the paper circles. Let dry. Spread glue on opposite side of the circles and gently pull the top layer of the honeycomb paper over and onto the opposite side of the circle. Glue the large circle to the stork and the small circles to the wheels of the baby carriage. Glue the stork and baby carriage on frame. Write name on banner and glue inside the stork bundle. Draw details on top of the bundle. Glue the bundle and banner on baby carriage. For center mat, cut a rectangle from blue cardstock and cut a circle from the center. To emboss mat, use a heart template and a stylus. Place photo behind mat and place in frame.

Design by Julie McGuffee for Accu Cut

Tree Top Angel

SUPPLIES

- White Cardstock
- White 6" round paper doily
- White 6" heart doily
- Accu-Cut die-cut: Angel #1B
- Pink 1/8" wide satin ribbon, 12 inches
- Translucent Glitter
- Paintbrush
- Elmer's Craft Bond Glue

INSTRUCTIONS

Cut the Angel from white paper. Carefully cut wings away from body to within 1/2" of head. Cut doily in half. Fold one half of doily into a cone shape around the angel body, sliding up to the head. Glue edges to the back of the body. With paintbrush, apply glue along the wings, halo, and doilies and sprinkle with glitter. Glue the heart doily on back of angel. Tie a bow with 8" of ribbon and glue at the neck. Cut ends at a slant. For hanger, insert ribbon through the halo and glue ends together. Cut the head of one of your own "little angels" from a photograph and glue in place.

Design by Julie McGuffee for Accu-Cut

Cincinnati Weekend

SUPPLIES

- Paper Pizazz: Yellow, purple paper (Plain Brights)
- Fiskars Paper Edger: Stamp
- ZIG MS marker: Black Writer
- Elmer's Craft Bond Glue Stick

INSTRUCTIONS

Make a "thanks for the hospitality" gift after a fun time together with friends. It's easy when you remember to take pictures! Once you see how much photo gifts are appreciated, you'll find yourself planning ahead to capture the shots that will be meaningful reminders of special times and events. You don't have to make an elaborate presentation. Remember the importance of the pictures.

Design by Julie Stephani for Krause Publications

Garden FRAME

SUPPLIES

- Green Cardstock
- Ready-to-Make frame
- ZIG MS markers: Writers - Black, green, gray
  Black Calligraphy Writer
  Green Scroll & Brush
  White fine-tip Opaque Writer
- Inkworx Air Art Gun
- Accu-Cut die-cuts: Small Banner #3
- Stickopotamus stickers: Mini flowers, outside accessories
- Paintbrush
- Decoupage Matte Finish
- Elmer's Craft Bond Glue

INSTRUCTIONS

Use the brush tip of the Scroll & Brush marker and the Inkworx to gently spray green onto the front of the frame. Use large end of the calligraphy marker to make check marks around the inside and outside edges of frame. Outline the edges of frame, using the large calligraphy tip. Place the center of the tip on the front edge of the frame and draw a line by pulling the marker toward you. The width of the line will be determined by the amount of pressure you exert on the marker. Place the fence stickers along the bottom of the frame. Outline the right side and top of the fence stickers with the gray Writer. Place the mini flower stickers around the front of the frame, leaving room between each one to write the saying. For leaves press the brush tip of the green Scroll and Brush marker onto the surface. Draw vines with the extra fine green Writer. Outline the edge of small banner with the fine black Writer. Highlight with the white Opaque writer. Glue banner on frame. Seal frame with two or three coats of decoupage matte finish.

Design by Julie McGuffee for Accu-Cut and EK Success

Papa & Me

On the scrapbook pages:

Papa AND ME

We are best friends.

He lets me steer!

Papa's Tractor

We wear matching shirts!

We pop·pop·pop popcorn together.

Lucky Garrett!

Lucky Papa!

I do whatever Papa does.

Look what we did!

Papa always has time to play with me.

SUPPLIES

- Paper Pizazz: Green, red, blue, yellow, purple (Plain Brights)
- Fiskars Paper Edger: Scallop
- ZIG MS marker: Black Writer
- Accu-Cut die-cuts: Tractor, letters
- Mrs. Grossman's stickers; Geometric shapes
- Elmer's Craft Bond Glue

INSTRUCTIONS

Collect pictures that reflect a special relationship between people. These pictures were taken over a few years and collected on two pages to give as a birthday gift for Papa. The little guy loved the pages so much that guess what he's getting for <u>his</u> birthday? Vary and overlap shapes of photos to get more pictures on the page. Notice the small squares used for accents on just one corner of two of the pictures. The large die-cut letters are fun to use when you only have a few short words. Accent letters, mats, and pages with dots and dashes.

Design by Julie Stephani for Krause Publications

Bess's Wish

Bess gets her wish

90 years young!

Into the heavens!

A wave before take off.

SUPPLIES

- ✤ Paper Pizazz: Cloud paper (Vacation)
    Blue, white paper
- ✤ Fiskars Paper Edger: Jigsaw
- ✤ Zig MS marker: Black Writer
- ✤ Elmer's Craft Bond Glue Stick

INSTRUCTIONS

Give a memory-page gift that captures a very special occasion. When a number of people want the same page, color copy the entire page rather than making each page from scratch. The photos on this page overlap and connect to each other for a layout that is simple but effective. Paper strips add color and direct the eye through the page.

Design by Julie Stephani for Krause Publications

Carol's Cursive

Aa Bb Cc Dd Ee
Ff Gg Hh Ii Jj Kk
Ll Mm Nn Oo Pp
Qq Rr Ss Tt Uu Vv
Ww Xx Yy Zz

Chapter 14: Celebrations

Dog Days

SUPPLIES

❖ Paper Pizazz: Orange paper (Plain Brights)
❖ Fiskars Paper Trimmer
❖ ZIG MS marker: Black Millenium, .03mm
❖ Mrs. Grossman's stickers:
    Dogs & Pups, Birthday Party, Sparkle
    Stars, Primary Design Lines, Basic Black
    & White Design Lines

❖ Thin red string
❖ Star cut-out
❖ Elmer's Craft Bond Glue

INSTRUCTIONS

Mat photos with 1/8" borders. Place Black & White Design Lines 1" from top and bottom edges of page. Place orange Primary Design Lines next to first ones. Place dogs on bottom border. Press crown on large black and gray dog.

Glue star and red string tied in a bow onto dog's neck Press funny glasses and nose on brown dog. Press dog biscuits around page. Add journaling.

Design by Andrea Grossman for Sticker Planet

Doggy Bags

SUPPLIES

❖ Sticker Planet gift bags
❖ Mrs. Grossman's stickers:
    Party Hats, Dogs & Pups, Checkerboard
    Plus Design Lines, Basic Red & White
    Design Lines

INSTRUCTIONS

Press three balloons on top of each bag. Trim around balloons. Press a sticker border across bag, 1" up from bottom. Press dog on border.

Decorate with party stickers and confetti.

Design by Heidi Geffen for Sticker Planet

Dress-Up Day

SUPPLIES

- ❖ Paper Pizazz: Red, yellow paper (Plain Brights)
- ❖ ZIG MS marker: Black Millenium, .05mm
- ❖ Accu-Cut die-cut: Dog House
- ❖ Mrs. Grossman's stickers
    - Dogs & Pups, Animal Expressions, Alphabet, Grass, Insects, Small Flowers, Party Hats, Multi-colored Confetti, Multi-colored Hearts, Airplane, Birthday Party, Checkerboard Plus Design Lines, Basic Red & White Design Lines, Pop-Dots
- ❖ Elmer's Craft Bond Glue Stick

INSTRUCTIONS

Press checkerboard border around edges. Add thin red polka-dot border along inside edge of first border. Silhouette photos of dog. Arrange photos in front of dog house or coming out of dog-house door. Once position of house is determined, glue door piece down first. Glue dog house, photo and bone die-cut on page.

Use alphabet stickers for title and dog's names. Add layers of sticker grass. Use pop-dots to give the grass dimension. Press sticker dogs, flowers, and insects on page. Draw squiggle dots on flies. Press dogs in pilots' seats and press one dog on each end of title. Add confetti.

Page design by Heidi Geffen, Sticker Planet

INVITATIONS

SUPPLIES

- ❖ Sticker Planet door hangers
- ❖ Mrs. Grossman's stickers:
    - Dogs & Pups
    - Birthday Party
    - Checkerboard Plus Design Lines
    - Basic Red & White Design Lines
- ❖ Invitation stamp
- ❖ Rainbow stamp pad

INSTRUCTIONS

Stamp invitation on center of each door hanger. Press Design Lines border approximately 1" from bottom of door hanger. Place dog on border. Decorate with confetti, balloons, party hats, etc.

Designed by Heidi Geffen, Sticker Planet

4th of July

SUPPLIES

✤ Paper Pizazz: Hearts, coils & stars paper
    (Childhood Memories)
    Yellow, green, blue, red, purple, orange
    paper (Plain Brights)
    Black paper (Solid Jewel Tones)
✤ Fiskars: Paper Edgers - Ripple
    Paper Punch - Star
✤ ZIG MS marker: Black Millennium
✤ Accu-Cut die-cut: Camera
✤ Mrs. Grossman's stickers: Border lines
✤ Elmer's Craft Bond Glue

INSTRUCTIONS

Brightly patterned paper will add fun to any album page. After cropping and matting the photos into different shapes, lay them on the page. With this 12" square page, there is room to add the border stickers along the middle of the page. The die-cut camera is a perfect embellishment for the event and a great place to journal. The punched stars (in two sizes) carry out the theme of a fun day.

Design by Becky Goughnour for Hot Off The Press

PARTY Invitation

SUPPLIES

✤ Paper Pizazz: Hearts, coils & stars paper
    (Childhood Memories)
    (optional for lining inside of envelope)
✤ ZIG MS markers: Fine & Chisel –Black,
    yellow, red, orange, green, blue, teal
✤ Blank card with window panes and envelope
✤ Stickopotamus stickers: Birthday Fun
✤ Elmer's Craft Bond Glue

INSTRUCTIONS

Crop and mount photo on invitation. With violet and red Fine & Chisel markers, letter invitation using "Parrothead" alphabet. Add doodle accents with other colors. Add swirls around outside of cropped photo and color in.

Print first name on envelope with "Parrothead" alphabet. Add stickers around address as shown. Cut a rectangle of birthday paper as a lining for envelope. Insert and glue inside envelope.

Spencer is three!

SUPPLIES

- Paper Pizazz: Party confetti paper (Birthday) White, red, blue, turquoise paper
- Fiskars Paper Edgers: Ripple, Mini Scallop
- ZIG MS markers: Fine & Chisel –Black, yellow, red, orange, green, blue, teal
- Foam adhesive spacers
- Paper Hole Punch
- 1" wide ribbon: Red, yellow, blue; 18 inches
- Elmer's Craft Bond Glue

INSTRUCTIONS

Cut party paper in half into two 8 1/2" x 5 1/2" pieces. Trim 3 sides of one piece with Ripple paper edgers. Mat on white piece of paper, placing straight cut down. With black Fine & Chisel marker, letter headline on white paper, using "Parrothead" alphabet. Add doodle accents with other colors. Mat headline on turquoise paper and trim with Mini Scallop paper edgers. Glue foam adhesive spacers to back of headline and position at top of page. For pocket, fold two corners of blue paper towards center so they almost meet, forming two triangular shapes. Fold remainder of paper down along top of triangles. For top pocket, trim excess piece of paper evenly at bottom edge of triangular points, about 2-1/2".

Cut two triangles of red paper the same size as blue triangles. Cut two squares of party paper to fit blue square under triangles. Trim each red triangle with Mini Scallop paper edgers. Trim each party square with Ripple paper edgers. Mat each red triangle on top of blue. Glue each birthday square on top of blue squares and underneath triangles. Punch a hole in each triangle at top through all layers. Thread ribbons through each hole and tie in a knot.

Cut a large triangle, 6" x 6" x 8-1/2" from red paper. Make a dot/dash line along the edges of all red triangles with black Fine & Chisel marker. Glue pieces on page from the bottom up. Place the red-topped triangles at the bottom, then the 2-1/2" strip of blue behind it, followed by the large red triangle. Arrange and glue red triangle down completely. Glue small blue strip (top pocket) and red-topped triangles (bottom pocket) only on the sides. Add doodle accents. Glue photo inside the bottom pocket.

DOOR HANGER

SUPPLIES

✤ Paper Pizazz : Hearts, coils & stars paper (Childhood Memories)
    Purple moiré paper
    White paper
✤ ZIG MS markers: Fine & Chisel –Violet, pink, yellow, 2 greens, blue
✤ Accu-Cut die-cut: Door Hanger
✤ Stickopotamus stickers: "Birthday Fun"
✤ Elmer's Craft Bond Glue

INSTRUCTIONS

Mount two colors of door hangers together back to back for stability. With violet Fine & Chisel marker, letter headline on white paper, using "Parrothead" alphabet. Add doodle accents with other colors. Glue headline on birthday paper, trimming a 1/4" border all around. Center and glue white piece on hanger. Add birthday stickers.

CANDY TOPPER
AND GIFT TAG

SUPPLIES

✤ Paper Pizazz: Hearts, coil & star paper (Childhood Memories)
    White, green paper
✤ Fiskars Paper Edger: Victorian
✤ ZIG MS markers: Fine & Chisel –yellow, red, orange, green, 2 blue
✤ Stickopotamus stickers: "Birthday Fun"
✤ Plastic bag and candies
✤ Elmer's Craft Bond Glue

INSTRUCTIONS

With blue Fine & Chisel marker, letter headline on white paper, using "Parrothead" alphabet. Add doodle accents with other colors. Add birthday sticker on side. Trim with Victorian paper edger. Mat headline on party paper and trim with Victorian paper edger. Mat on a doubled piece of green paper. Fill a small snack size plastic bag with candies. Wrap candy topper around bag and glue or staple closed.

SUPPLIES

✤ Paper Pizazz: Yellow paper
✤ ZIG MS markers: Fine & Chisel –Violet, red, orange, green, teal
✤ Accu-Cut die-cut: Scroll Gift Tag
✤ Stickopotamus stickers: "Birthday Fun"
✤ Elmer's Craft Bond Glue

INSTRUCTIONS

With violet Fine & Chisel marker, letter headline on scalloped front and flap of gift tag, using "Parrothead" alphabet. Add doodle accents with other colors. Press birthday sticker on side.

Birthday Card

SUPPLIES

- ❖ Paper Pizazz: Hearts, coils & stars paper (Childhood Memories)
- ❖ White, yellow, blue, pink, fuchsia paper
- ❖ Fiskars: Paper Edgers - Seagull
- ❖ Paper Crimper
- ❖ ZIG MS markers: Fine & Chisel –Black, red, yellow, orange, blue, green
- ❖ Elmer's Craft Bond Glue

INSTRUCTIONS

Run scraps of solid colors through the Paper Crimper and cut into 1/4" wide strips. Some strips will be larger than card. With red Fine & Chisel marker, letter headline on white paper, using "Parrothead" alphabet. Add doodle accents with other colors. Trim entire headline with Seagull paper edger. Glue headline on card over crimped strips.

MAGIC WAND

SUPPLIES

- ❖ White cardstock
- ❖ Fiskars Paper Edger: Victorian
- ❖ ZIG MS markers: Fine & Chisel –Black, yellow, red, orange, green, blue, teal
- ❖ White card stock
- ❖ Plastic balloon stick
- ❖ 1" wide sheer ribbon: blue, red, yellow; 1 yard each
- ❖ Elmer's Craft Bond Glue

INSTRUCTIONS

Cut two 6" circles from white card stock. Crop and mount photo onto one circle. Trim both circles with Victorian paper edger.
With black Fine & Chisel marker, letter head-line using "Parrothead". Add doodle accents with other colors. Add swirls around outside of circle and color in.

Party Collection Designs by Lindsay Ostrom for EK Success

Parrothead

Behind the Scenes

Director Ivy Chapman (left) makes her calls from the control room.

Directions and changes are discussed between takes.

Andrea, Michele, Suzy, and Julie take time out for a group hug!

The Memory Experts

Sandy Cashman
Fiskars, Inc.

Jennie Dayley
Stickopotamus

Heidi Geffen
Sticker Planet

Michele Gerbrandt
Memory Makers

Andrea Grossman
Mrs. Grossman's Paper Co.

Paulette Jarvey
Hot Off The Press, Inc.

Stacy Jullian
Creating Keepsakes

Jean Kievlan
Accu-Cut

Deanna Lambson
Creating Keepsakes

Diane Yokes adjusts Jennie's makeup and hairstyle for the camera lights.

Tammy goes over her notes before going on the set.

Julie and Jean show off the die-cuts that were made in their segment.

Keeping track of wardrobe keeps Deanna and Stacy on their toes!

Julie
McGuffee
Accu-Cut

Tammy
Muto
*Delta
Technical
Coatings*

Toni
Nelson
*EK
Success*

Beth
Reames
*EK
Success*

Carol
Snyder
*EK
Success*

Suzy
Spafford
Suzy's Zoo

Bill
Stephani
*Great
American
Crafts*

Julie
Stephani
*Great
American
Crafts*

Glossary

ACID FREE

Acid is used in paper manufacturing to break apart the wood fibers and the lignin which holds them together. If acid remains in the materials used for photo albums, the acid can react chemically with photographs and accelerate their deterioration. Acid-free products have a pH factor of 7 to 8.5. It's imperative that all materials (glue, pens, paper, etc.) used in memory albums or scrapbooks be acid free.

ACID MIGRATION

Acid Migration is the transfer of acidity from one item to another through physical contact or acidic vapors. If a newspaper clipping was put into an album, the area it touched would turn yellow or brown. A de-acidification spray can be used on acidic papers, or they can be color photocopied onto acid-free papers.

BUFFERED PAPER

During manufacturing a buffering agent such as calcium carbonate or magnesium bicarbonate can be added to paper to neutralize acid contaminants. Such papers have a pH of 8.5.

CROPPING

Cropping is cutting or trimming a photo to keep only the most important parts.

DIE-CUTS

Precut paper shapes used to decorate pages.

JOURNALING

Journaling refers to the text on an album page giving details about the photographs. It can be done in your own handwriting or with adhesive letters, rub-ons, etc. It is one of the most important parts of memory albums because it tells the story behind the photos.

LIGNIN

Lignin is the bonding material which holds wood fibers together as a tree grows. If lignin remains in the final paper product (as with newsprint), it will become yellow and brittle over time. Most paper other than newsprint is lignin free.

MATTING

Background paper used to frame and enhance the photo image.

pH FACTOR

The pH factor refers to the acidity of a paper. The pH scale is the standard for measurement of acidity and alkalinity. It runs from 0 to 14 with each number representing a ten-fold increase. pH neutral is 7. Acid-free products have a pH factor from 7 to 8.5. Special pH tester pens are available to help determine the acidity or alkalinity of products.

PHOTO SAFE

This is a term similar to "archival quality" but more specific to materials used with photographs. Acid-free is the determining factor for a product to be labeled photo safe.

SHEET PROTECTORS

These are made of plastic to slip over a finished album page. They can be side-loading or top-loading and fit 8-1/2" x 11" pages or 12" x 12" sheets. It is important that they be acid-free. Polypropylene is commonly used. Never use vinyl sheet protectors.

Reprinted from
Making Great Scrapbook Pages
Hot Off the Press, Inc.